Ethics-in-Government Laws
Are They Too "Ethical"?

Alfred S. Neely IV

American Enterprise Institute for Public Policy Research
Washington and London

Alfred S. Neely IV is Edward W. Hinton Professor of Law at the University of Missouri–Columbia School of Law, a public trustee of the Food and Drug Law Institute, and a consultant to the Administrative Conference of the United States.

The author would like to acknowledge and express appreciation for the research assistance of Deborah J. Neff and Mark D. Dopp, students at the University of Missouri–Columbia School of Law.

Library of Congress Cataloging in Publication Data
Neely, Alfred S.
    Ethics-in-government laws.

    (AEI studies ; 402)
    Includes bibliographical references.
1. Conflict of interests (Public office)—United
States. I. Title. II. Series.
KF4568.N43   342.73'0684   84-3033
            347.302684

ISBN 0–8447–3550–7

1 3 5 7 9 10 8 6 4 2

AEI Studies 402

Printed in the United States of America

Contents

Foreword

Coming in a presidential election year, the release of this study on the ethics-in-government laws is particularly timely. After an election many people in the private sector consider making a transition into public service. According to the author, Alfred S. Neely IV, ethics-in-government laws influence decisions to accept or reject government positions and, ultimately, affect the character and quality of the government itself.

Although everyone favors ethical conduct in governmental affairs, the laws intended to effect it involve costs as well as benefits. They may discourage excellent people from entering government, Neely concludes. He gives us hypothetical case studies that show the effects of these laws on incumbent and potential public officials.

This study will help the reader evaluate the public policy issues underlying ethics-in-government laws. Readers contemplating service in the federal government will find this book a special aid in weighing the advantages and disadvantages of such service.

This book has been prepared under the auspices of AEI's Legal Policy Studies Program as one of several AEI publications on the juncture of ethics and public policy. They include *Regulating International Business through Codes of Conduct*, by Raymond J. Waldman, and *Proposed Revisions of the Foreign Corrupt Practices Act*, a legislative analysis. Other AEI study centers have also addressed ethical issues. AEI's Center for Hemispheric Studies, for example, has published Howard Wiarda's *Human Rights and U.S. Human Rights Policy*, and AEI's Center for Studies in Religion, Philosophy, and Public Policy has published Bernard Murchland's *Humanism and Capitalism: A Survey of Thought on Morality and the Economic Order* and many others.

The competition of ideas, we believe, is fundamental to a free society. Certainly this is no less true in ethics than in any other aspect of public policy.

WILLIAM J. BAROODY, JR.
President
American Enterprise Institute

1
Introduction

No American public official has a uniform, but all receive salaries. This . . . is the result of democratic principles. A democracy could surround its magistrates with pomp, covering them in silk and gold, without making any direct attack on the principle of its existence. Such privileges are ephemeral, going with the place rather than with the man. But to establish unpaid official positions is to create a class of rich and independent functionaries and to shape the core of an aristocracy. Even if the people still retain the right of choice, the exercise of that right comes to have inevitable limitations.

When a democratic republic converts salaried appointments into unpaid ones, I think one may conclude that it is steering toward monarchy. And when a monarchy begins paying its unsalaried officials, that is a sure sign that it is working either toward a despotic or toward a republican condition.

I therefore think that the change from salaried to unpaid appointments by itself constitutes a real revolution.

I regard the complete absence of unpaid duties as one of the clearest indications of democracy's absolute sway in America. The public pays for all services of whatever sort performed in its interest; hence any man has the chance as well as the right to perform them.[1]

TOCQUEVILLE, *Democracy in America*

These observations by Alexis de Tocqueville concerned America in the first half of the nineteenth century. Yet, as is so often the case, his insights travel well. Today compensation in return for public service continues to be a trait of public life in America, and presumably the likelihood of Tocqueville's "real revolution" remains remote. Nevertheless, there are persistent reports of persons who decline public positions or leave them prematurely because of inadequate compensation. To the extent that this is or becomes a major phenomenon, inadequate compensation may have the same effect as none at all on the character and quality of public life.

1

The purpose here is not to analyze and debate the adequacy of compensation in public life. Tocqueville's commentary serves, however, to highlight a point of obvious and fundamental importance: economics may play as important a role as devotion to the public good in a decision to accept or reject a public position. Indeed, this led Tocqueville to the conclusion that "in the United States it is men of moderate pretensions who engage in the twists and turns of politics. Men of . . . vaulting ambition generally avoid power to pursue wealth; the frequent result is that men undertake to direct the fortunes of the state only when they doubt their capacity to manage their private affairs."[2] One need not be so harsh to accept the view that the economics of public service may often prove a deterrent to persons who are otherwise able and willing to serve.

There may be barriers to public service other than direct remuneration that are less obvious and dramatic but are still essentially economic. Ethics-in-government laws are one possible source of such barriers.

In general it would seem that there can never be a surplus of ethics in the conduct of governmental affairs. This perception may arise especially where there is real or potential competition between the personal inclinations and interests of a public servant and notions of the public interest. In such cases the high value placed on ethics in government dictates subordination of personal interests to the public interest. This is understandable inasmuch as it is both philosophically and politically expedient to equate the highest standards of ethical conduct with the highest standards of good government.

During the 1970s, particularly in the post-Watergate era, there arose an intense and resurgent interest in ethics in government. This was reflected in the passage of the Ethics in Government Act of 1978, which, among other things, created a new Office of Government Ethics.[3] The interest was not confined to the public sector. Bar associations, for example, devoted considerable time and effort to ethical standards for attorneys with past or present government service.[4]

The purpose of this study is to examine various facets and implications of federal ethics-in-government laws. The premise is not and should not be that ethical conduct in governmental affairs is not a worthy and desirable objective. A premise that does merit examination, however, is that ethics-in-government laws are not without costs, which must be identified and weighed in the balance against their benefits. It may well be that the marginal costs of additional limits on those in or considering government service are such that those limits are difficult to justify in light of their overall effect on the nature and quality of government. If so, greater ethical con-

2

straints in government may not necessarily produce better government in the long run.

There is reason to believe that ethics-in-government laws create potential barriers to entry into, exit from, and consequently excellence in the federal public service. If this is so, it may be time for reexamination and refinement of those laws to make certain that their costs are fully understood and appreciated when measured against their benefits. The ultimate objective should be to ensure that whatever balance is struck between these interests is reflected accurately in the ethics-in-government laws.

The varieties of ostensibly ethical constraints on government service are numerous. Here, however, the focus is not on the propriety of entertainment of government officials while in office or of a gift of a turkey at Thanksgiving. Nor is it on blatant bribery of public officials, although these are important as background and contrast and are examined to some extent. Rather, the concern here is with the ethical constraints of less obvious and compelling force that may have the effect of inhibiting entry into or exit from government service.

Notes

1. Alexis de Tocqueville, *Democracy in America* (New York: J. Mayer and M. Lerner, 1966), pp. 188–89.

2. Ibid., p. 189.

3. See section "The Ethics in Government Act of 1978," in chap. 2.

4. See section "Executive Orders and Agency Regulations," in chap. 2.

2
Present Federal
Ethics-in-Government Laws

There are several sources of ethical constraints on federal public service. The purpose of this chapter is to introduce the reader to them to facilitate appreciation of the subsequent discussion of the effect of the present system on various target populations.

Title 18 of the U.S. Code

Sensitivity to the need for legal constraints to further the objective of ethical government is not a discovery of the decade just passed. Much of chapter 11 of Title 18 of the U.S. Code antedates the 1970s. And, not insignificantly, that chapter, "Bribery, Graft, and Conflicts of Interest," appears in a title devoted exclusively to crimes and criminal procedure.

These statutory provisions present an array of restraints concerning conduct while in and after leaving public office. Such restraints may also restrain entry because an informed and rational person can be expected to weigh them in making the decision to accept or reject public employment. Generally, however, there are no express preemployment restraints before the time at which a person takes office or, at least, has been nominated, appointed, or officially informed of impending nomination or appointment.[1]

These restraints on the conduct of public officials while in office are generally neither unexpected nor untoward. Overall, they serve salutary public purposes and accepted norms for public life. Thus bribery of public officials for the purpose of influencing official acts, the commission of frauds on the United States, or the inducement of acts in violation of lawful duties is prohibited.[2] The clear objective of the prohibition of bribery is to safeguard the integrity of government and prevent its corruption;[3] it is not likely to lead to protracted debate in responsible circles. It is quite reasonable for the government to make every effort to discourage, for example, financial transactions

4

between a private accountant and an Internal Revenue Service auditor when the purpose of the transaction is to influence the auditor's decision concerning the accountant's clients.[4]

Similar motives are reflected in the more specific statutory provisions barring loans or gratuities to bank examiners,[5] undisclosed consideration in connection with procurement of loans or credit from Federal Reserve banks,[6] and the receipt of commissions or gifts in connection with loans from federally related financial institutions.[7] The thrust of the bribery prohibitions is to preclude direct yet external financial interference in the performance of public duties. The underlying philosophy is that the public servant is to have but one master.

For similar reasons officers and employees of the United States are prohibited from acting as agents for a foreign principal.[8] And they are not permitted to receive compensation, except as provided by law, for services "in relation to any proceeding, application, request for a ruling or other determination, contract, claim, controversy, charge, accusation, arrest, or other particular matter in which the United States is a party or has a direct and substantial interest, before any department, agency, courtmartial, officer, or any civil, military, or naval commission."[9] This is generally consistent with the theme of "one master," especially in the context of compensation in relation to specific affairs of government. The appearance, even if not the fact, of improper influence in such situations would seem to justify the harsh treatment afforded under the statute. In the same vein officers and employees of the United States, with a few exceptions, may not act as agents or attorneys in prosecuting claims against the United States or in proceedings before various agencies and governmental bodies.[10]

A broader and fundamentally different prohibition concerns the permissible sources of compensation for services as an officer or employee of the executive branch or of an independent agency. The difference is that the bar is not tied to any particular governmental action or proceeding. Such a person may not receive "any salary, or any contribution to or supplementation of salary, as compensation for his services as an officer or employee of the executive branch . . . [or] of any independent agency . . . , from any source other than the Government of the United States, except as may be contributed out of the treasury of any State, county, or municipality."[11] There are, nevertheless, a few additional exceptions to this prohibition. Continued participation in various benefit plans maintained by a former employer, such as pension and retirement programs, is allowed.[12] Nor does the prohibition apply to an officer or employee serving without compensation;[13] and for executive exchange or fellowship programs in an executive agency, an exception is made for actual relocation expenses paid by persons other than the government, if the program is established by statute or executive order.[14]

The prohibitions of Title 18 extend in other ways to the personal financial interests of officers and employees of the executive branch and the independent agencies. Generally, such persons may not participate

> personally and substantially . . . through decision, approval, disapproval, recommendation, the rendering of advice, investigation, or otherwise, in a judicial or other proceeding, application, request for a ruling or other determination, contract, claim, controversy, charge, accusation, arrest, or other particular matter in which, to his knowledge, he, his spouse, minor child, partner, organization in which he is serving as officer, director, trustee, partner or employee, or any person or organization with whom he is negotiating or has any arrangement concerning prospective employment, has a financial interest.[15]

A person whose personal financial interests are otherwise within the purview of this provision may obtain relief from the possibility of liability if she first informs the official responsible for her appointment of the matter that creates the apparent conflict, makes full disclosure of the financial interest, and receives prior written determination that "the interest is not so substantial as to be deemed likely to affect the integrity of the services which the Government may expect from such officer or employee."[16] Individual determination of these issues may not be necessary if the financial interest has been exempted by rule published in the *Federal Register* declaring the interest too inconsequential or remote to affect the integrity of the person's services.[17]

The principal Title 18 provision pertaining to officers and employees of the executive branch and the independent agencies once they leave government service is comprehensive and complex.

First, the former employee may not act as attorney or agent for or otherwise represent anyone by way of formal or informal appearance before, or oral or written communication to, the government in any matter in which the United States is a party or has a substantial and direct interest if the matter is one in which the former employee "participated personally and substantially as an officer or employee through decision, approval, disapproval, recommendation, the rendering of advice, investigation or otherwise, while so employed."[18] The prohibition applies to the same wide array of matters covered by the personal financial interest provision quoted previously.

Second, a more limited and simultaneously expansive prohibition concerns certain activities within two years after the former employee has left government service. A former employee is prohibited from making formal or informal appearances or oral or written communications on behalf of others in any matter "which was actually pending under his official responsibility as an officer or employee within a period of one year prior to termination of such responsibility, or . . . in which he participated personally and substantially as an officer or employee."[19] Furthermore, certain high-level officials who held positions typically involving significant decision-making or supervisory responsibility[20] may not "knowingly represent, aid, counsel, advise, consult or assist in representing any other person by personal presence at any formal or informal appearance"[21] in any such matter during the two-year period.

A further limitation on the activities of former high-ranking officials precludes any representation for one year after leaving the government in any formal or informal appearances before, or oral or written communications to, the department or agency in which the former employee served in connection with any matter in which the department or agency has a direct and substantial interest.[22]

There are certain limited exceptions to some of these prohibitions. The one-year bar does not apply if the former employee moves on to elected state or local office or to employment by a state or local agency, an institution of higher learning, or a hospital or medical research organization and his dealings with his former department or agency are on behalf of his new employer.[23] And no former employee, no matter who is his new employer, is prevented from making appearances or communications "of a personal and individual nature."[24]

None of the limitations mentioned apply under certain circumstances "with respect to the making of communications solely for the purpose of furnishing scientific or technological information."[25] The statute also does not prevent the sworn testimony or statements of the former employee.[26]

The prohibition against acting as agent or attorney on behalf of anyone in a matter in which an officer or employee "participates or has participated personally and substantially as an officer or employee through decision, approval, disapproval, recommendation, the rendering of advice, investigation, or otherwise, or which is the subject of his official responsibility"[27] is not confined to the officer or employee alone, but extends to any partner.

7

Under Title 18 a number of sanctions are available to encourage compliance. The most obvious and probably best recognized is the range of possible criminal penalties—fine, imprisonment, or both—but there are others. The president or his properly authorized delegate at the head of the department or agency involved

> may declare void and rescind any contract, loan, grant, subsidy, license, right, permit, franchise, use, authority, privilege, benefit, certificate, ruling, decision, opinion, or rate schedule awarded, granted, paid, furnished, or published, or the performance of any service or transfer or delivery of anything to, by or for any agency of the United States or officer or employee of the United States or person acting on behalf thereof, in relation to which there has been a final conviction for any violation of this chapter, and the United States shall be entitled to recover in addition to any penalty prescribed by law or in a contract the amount expended or the thing transferred or delivered on its behalf, or the reasonable value thereof.[28]

There are also essentially civil prospective sanctions. If the head of a department or agency finds, after notice and an opportunity for a hearing, that a former officer or employee has violated one of the statutory provisions governing the conduct of such persons with respect to governmental matters, the former officer or employee may be barred from representing others before the agency for as long as five years.[29]

The ethics-in-government philosophy reflected by Title 18 is prohibitory. An effort has been made to specify prohibited acts and ensure compliance through a variety of sanctions. As the following discussion of the Ethics in Government Act of 1978 reveals, there are other and quite different approaches to the issue.

The Ethics in Government Act of 1978

The hallmark of the Ethics in Government Act of 1978 is its reliance on public disclosure as a means of ensuring that public rather than private purposes are served in public life. One of the act's titles establishes financial disclosure requirements for personnel in the executive branch.[30]

Those requirements apply from the highest levels—the president and vice president—through the executive branch generally to persons classified as at least GS-16.[31] All such persons must file a report containing the prescribed information within thirty days of assuming office. The report must be submitted even earlier in cases requiring

Senate confirmation and within five days of the president's transmittal of the nomination. Candidates for president and vice president must submit reports within thirty days of becoming candidates.[32] Such reports must be filed annually while in office.[33]

The nature and extent of the information the reports must contain deserve close scrutiny not only by those directly affected but also by those interested in their potential effect on prospective and incumbent officeholders.

Except for income from current employment with the government, the source, type, and amount or value of income from any source must be disclosed. This includes the source, date, and amount of any honorariums aggregating $100 or more in value.[34] Dividends, rents, interest, and capital gains need not be disclosed in such detail; although the source and type of income must be shown, the amounts may be indicated within specified ranges, such as "greater than $5,000 but not more than $15,000."[35]

Any gifts of transportation, lodging, food, or entertainment aggregating more than $250 from a source other than a relative are subject to reporting; however, they are excluded if received as "personal hospitality of an individual," and gifts worth less than $35 need not be included. All other gifts aggregating more than $100 from sources other than a relative must be reported, with the same exception for smaller gifts.[36] If reimbursements aggregating more than $250 are received from any source, the source's identity and a brief description must be included.[37]

If the person subject to reporting has any interest in property in a trade or business, or property held for investment or production of income, with a fair market value greater than $1,000, the identity and category of value of the interest or property must be disclosed. Personal debts of relatives and personal saving accounts of less than $5,000 are excluded.[38]

The identity and category of value of liabilities greater than $10,000 owed to a creditor other than a relative must be reported, except for mortgages on personal residences and certain loans secured by personal property. Reporting persons need not be concerned with revolving charge accounts unless the liability exceeds $10,000, although then there may well be cause for concern wholly independent of the act.[39]

Transactions in real property, other than a personal residence, and in securities that exceed $1,000 must also be reported unless the other party to the transaction is the reporting person's spouse or dependent child.[40]

A report must list positions held during the reporting year and,

9

if it is a first report, during the preceding two years. No disclosure is required concerning honorary positions or those held in religious, social, fraternal, or political organizations; but it is required for positions as an officer, director, trustee, partner, proprietor, representative, employee, or consultant of any business enterprise, nonprofit organization, labor organization, or educational or other institution.[41]

Subject to protections for confidential information, nonelected reporting persons must also disclose for the two preceding calendar years all sources of compensation greater than $5,000 and a brief description of the duties performed.[42]

A variety of agreements and arrangements are within the reporting requirements. The date, parties, and terms of them with respect to future employment, leaves of absence during government service, continuation payments by a former employer, and continuing participation in an employee benefit or welfare plan of a former employer must be reported.[43]

Furthermore, the required information is not confined to the affairs of the reporting person. With some modest contraction, much of the same information is required about the financial status of spouses and dependent children.[44]

Trusts receive special and extensive consideration under the act. The same basic information that a reporting person must provide about other financial affairs must be disclosed with respect to the holdings and income of a trust from which he, his spouse, or his dependent child receives income or holds a beneficial interest. An exception is made for the holdings of a trust not created by the reporting person, his spouse, or his dependent child when they have no knowledge of the holdings or sources of income of the trust, although the category of the amount of income received must still be reported.[45] The same is true of a special creation of the act, the qualified blind trust.

For a trust to be "qualified," the trustee must meet certain conditions whose objective is to ensure his independence from persons with an interest in the trust. The assets of the trust generally must be free of restrictions on their sale or transfer. Furthermore, under the terms of the trust instrument the trustee must be divorced from the control of the interested party, and the interested party must be insulated from all but the most general and innocuous information concerning the activities and holdings of the trust.[46]

The qualified blind trust is not a wholly private arrangement. The act created the Office of Government Ethics,[47] which must approve any proposed trust instrument and the proposed trustee.[48]

There are also continuing responsibilities to notify the Office of Government Ethics of various trust activities through the time at which the trust might be dissolved.[49]

Knowing and willful violations of the act's requirements may incur civil penalties up to $5,000, and negligent violations may incur civil penalties of as much as $1,000.[50]

Once received, the reports must be reviewed by designated government officials who decide whether the reporting person is in compliance with applicable laws and regulations. The individual may be notified of any steps considered necessary to ensure compliance, which may include divestiture, restitution, the establishment of a blind trust, or a voluntary request for transfer, reassignment, limitation of duties, or resignation.[51]

Reports filed pursuant to the act are not merely private matters between the reporting person and his employer, the United States government. With limited exceptions to accommodate the national interest, the reports must be made available to the public and retained for six years.[52]

Although the dominant philosophy of the act seems to be one of disclosure, aspects of its requirements go beyond disclosure and purport to structure and restructure the personal financial affairs of affected officers and employees. This is perhaps nowhere more evident than in the provision limiting the outside earned income of all employees in nonjudicial full-time positions who are at the level of GS-16 or above and who are appointed by the president. These employees' outside earned income may not exceed 15 percent of their salaries.[53]

The preceding discussion of provisions of the Ethics in Government Act is perhaps too detailed for some readers. Yet it is necessary background for an appreciation of much that follows. For the moment, however, even the reader who is not and never expects or wants to be subject to these requirements might pause to reflect on what effect they might have on a decision to accept a government post.

Executive Orders and Agency Regulations

Ethics-in-government requirements today are found not only in statutes but also in other governmental pronouncements, principally presidential executive orders and agency rules and regulations.

In 1965 President Lyndon B. Johnson issued Executive Order No. 11222, "Standards of Ethical Conduct for Government Officers and Employees."[54] Relying on its own terms and on required and

11

anticipated regulations of the Civil Service Commission and individual agencies for implementation, the order addresses at some length standards of conduct and reporting requirements for financial interests. These, of course, are some of the same matters included under the Title 18 prohibitions and today under the Ethics in Government Act; however, inasmuch as Title 18 is set in a criminal law context in which intent and corrupt motive often play important roles, a provision of the executive order often presents a more absolute and effective bar.

The order prohibits the direct or indirect solicitation or acceptance of a gift, gratuity, favor, entertainment, loan, or anything else of monetary value from anyone who has or seeks "contractual or other business or financial relationships" with the employee's agency, from anyone who "conducts operations or activities which are regulated" by the agency, and from anyone who has "interests which may be substantially affected by the performance or nonperformance of [the employee's] official duty."[55] The order does hold out the prospect of relief by agency regulation if necessary and appropriate in light of the agency's mission and the employee's duties.[56] Food and refreshments provided in the course of an inspection tour, for example, might be excepted.

In these provisions the intention and expectation were to ensure that employees avoid even the appearance of the use of public office for private gain, preferential treatment, loss of independence or partiality, decision making outside official channels, or adverse effects on public confidence in the integrity of government.[57]

The use of federal property for activities other than those officially approved or the use of official information not available to the general public to further a private interest is prohibited.[58] Employment outside the government is not prohibited. Activities such as teaching, lecturing, and writing are generally encouraged, but outside employment must not result in a real or apparent conflict of interest.[59]

Some essentially private matters are also addressed in the order. First, it makes clear that employees are "expected to meet all just financial obligations, especially those—such as Federal, State, or local taxes—which are imposed by law."[60] Second, employees are required to avoid substantial conflicts, real or apparent, between direct and indirect private interests and their official duties and responsibilities. Yet, subject to further limitations by individual agencies, employees are left "free to engage in lawful financial transactions to the same extent as private citizens."[61]

Concerning the reporting of financial interests, the order requires that the head of each agency, each presidential appointee in the Office of the President not subordinate to an agency head in that office, and each full-time member of a committee, board, or commission appointed by the president submit to the Civil Service Commission various personal and financial information.[62] The commission could extend the requirements to any employees of the heads of agencies.[63] The requirements of the order about the contents of the statement largely repeat today's requirements under the Ethics in Government Act and are therefore effectively superseded; one important difference, however, is that the general rule under the order is one of confidentiality of content except for good cause.[64]

The authority and obligations of the Civil Service Commission under the order now reside in the Office of Personnel Management, and in 1978 appropriate redesignations were incorporated in the order.[65] Today there are extensive regulations, promulgated by the Office of Government Ethics in the Office of Personnel Management, dealing with financial disclosure requirements for executive personnel, employee responsibilities and conduct, postemployment conflict of interest, and procedures.[66] These implement both the 1978 act and Executive Order No. 11222.

In addition to the comprehensive Office of Government Ethics regulations, many agencies have their own rules on the subject. These include the Federal Trade Commission, the Department of Defense, the General Services Administration, the Department of Labor, the Securities and Exchange Commission, the Department of Energy, and the Department of Agriculture.[67]

Discussion of specific aspects of both the comprehensive and the individual agency regulations will be deferred; elements of these will be brought to bear in the case studies in the next chapter. For the moment it should be sufficient for the reader to be aware of their existence as an important adjunct to the statutes and executive orders that permeate the ethics-in-government field.

Ethical Standards for Licensed Professionals as De Facto Federal Law

Theoretically the exclusive source of federal controls over the ethical conduct of federal officers and employees is the government itself. All the controls discussed in the preceding sections of this chapter—statutes, executive orders, and administrative rules and regulations—have this common source. Restraints on the conduct and affairs of those in government may also arise from sources entirely outside the government, which nevertheless have effects hardly distinguishable from those of governmental origin and thus constitute de facto federal ethics-in-government laws. The most conspicuous example concerns attorneys in government, a group of licensed professionals who are subject not only to federal ethics-in-government laws but also to codes of professional responsibility established in most instances by the various bar associations to which they belong or the courts before which they practice.

The relevance of these codes to the government attorney arises in a number of contexts. First is their bearing on an attorney's actual duties on the government's behalf. It has been suggested that the issue most often presented in this area is one of "conflicts of function" when conflicts arise "among the simultaneous functions and responsibilities imposed upon many attorneys in government."[68] Second, conflicts may arise with personal interests of the attorney. These may concern opportunities for outside employment while in government service and employment after departure from the government. In the latter context an especially important issue is presented. Whether the disqualification of the former government attorney from representation of certain persons or any persons in certain matters extends to other attorneys with whom the attorney is associated may affect the desirability of association with him. It is this second category of issues that is most pertinent to the question whether bar association standards constitute barriers to entry and exit for those who provide legal representation to the federal government.

Canon 9 of the American Bar Association's Code of Professional Responsibility provides: "A lawyer should avoid even the appearance of professional impropriety."[69] This provision has been thought to have special relevance to the government lawyer.

> Public confidence in government . . . requires that the lawyer consider not only the objective propriety of his conduct, but also the appearance it will present to an independent observer. This . . . concern is the principal reason for the special importance of Canon 9 . . . in the government context. The public's confidence in government is to a great extent determined by the reputation for honesty of the government's employees. Moreover, potentially improper conduct on the part of a government employee is more likely to be scrutinized by the public than that of a private attorney. This is not surprising, since the public is most concerned with the potential misuse of information and power gained when the public itself, rather than a private party, is suffering the consequences. Thus, an appearance of im-

propriety on the part of a government attorney will inevitably harm not only the individual attorney, but also the entire system of government that allows such improprieties to take place. A perceived impropriety by the former is inevitably seen as a fault of both.[70]

Canon 9 and this underlying intent may affect the government attorney's activities on behalf of the government, but they may also color an assessment of the propriety of the attorney's personal activities while in government employment and after leaving it.

It is important to note that these professional standards may have the effect of extending traditional federal limits on official conduct. In one case a federal district court found that an attorney who represented a client before his own agency had transgressed the ethical standard prohibiting the appearance of impropriety even if his conduct did not violate the relevant provision in Title 18.[71]

There are professional disciplinary rules that add specificity to the generality of the canons, and two, D.R. 9-101(B) and D.R. 5-105(D), illustrate the difficulties professional standards can create for the former government attorney. D.R. 9-101(B) provides that a lawyer "shall not accept private employment in a matter in which he had substantial responsibility while he was a public employee."[72] This provision is not without interpretive difficulty: what constitutes a "matter" and what constitutes a "substantial responsibility" must be determined. These issues need not prove overwhelming, however, although the higher the former employee in the hierarchy, the stronger the implication that he was responsible for everything within his governmental domain. Rather the cause for significant concern arises from the fact that upon leaving the government few attorneys "hang out a shingle" as sole practitioners. This is the point at which D.R. 5-105(D) has created considerable uncertainty.

D.R. 5-105(D) provides that "if a lawyer is required to decline employment or to withdraw from employment under a Disciplinary Rule, no partner, or associate, or any other lawyer affiliated with him or his firm, may accept or continue such employment."[73] A literal reading of the rule leads inexorably to the conclusion that any grounds for disqualification of a former or a present government attorney must result in disqualification of all other attorneys with whom he is affiliated. A prospective employer of a departing government attorney, faced with the choice between abandoning a major client and not hiring the attorney, would probably choose to stay with the client—a decision, it should be noted, that could be based on professional obligation to the client as much as on economic reality.

Uncertainty about whether the disciplinary rules meant what they appeared to say and apprehension about the consequences if they did led to a request for a formal ethics opinion from the American Bar Association. The 1975 opinion was sympathetic to the difficulties raised by a literal interpretation of the rules.

> There are . . . weighty policy considerations in support of the view that a special disciplinary rule relating only to former government lawyers should not broadly limit the lawyer's employment after he leaves government service. Some of the considerations favoring a construction of the rule in a manner not to restrict unduly the lawyer's future are the following: the ability of government to recruit young professionals and competent lawyers should not be interfered with by imposition of harsh restraints upon future practice nor should too great a sacrifice be demanded of the lawyers willing to enter government service; the rule serves no worthwhile public interest if it becomes a mere tool enabling a litigant to improve his prospects by depriving his opponent of competent counsel; and the rule should not be permitted to interfere needlessly with the rights of litigants to obtain competent counsel of their own choosing, particularly in specialized areas requiring special technical training and experience.[74]

A sensitivity to the needs of both government and subsequent clients for competent counsel thus produced an opinion that did not insist on literalism and absolute vicarious disqualification of all with whom the former government attorney might become affiliated. As the opinion concluded:

> An inflexible extension of disqualification throughout an entire firm would thwart those purposes. So long as the individual lawyer is held to be disqualified and is screened from any direct or indirect participation in the matter, the problem of his switching sides is not present; by contrast, an inflexible extension of disqualification throughout the firm often would result in real hardship to a client if complete withdrawal was mandated, because substantial work may have been completed regarding specific litigation prior to the time the government employee joined the partnership, or the client may have relied in the past on representation by the firm.[75]

An effort had been made to reach an accommodation.

Yet any impression the opinion gives that this "revolving door" issue has been resolved would be overoptimistic and misleading. The controversy and attendant uncertainty have continued.

A committee of the American Bar Association has been working for some time on a comprehensive revision of the ethical standards for lawyers. This group, the Kutak Commission, has progressed to the point of a proposed final draft of the association's Model Rules of Professional Conduct.[76] A number of its facets could have significant effects on government attorneys and the professional standards they must satisfy.

Under these rules any lawyer who has represented a client in a matter is not to represent another "in the same or a substantially related matter in which that client's interests are materially adverse to the interests of the former client unless the former client consents after disclosure consultation."[77] This rule would of course apply to the former government attorney, but it does not rely on the appearance-of-impropriety test of Canon 9 and may thus afford somewhat greater latitude.[78]

The problem of imputed disqualification remains. Rule 1.10(a) provides that "when lawyers are associated in a firm, none of them shall knowingly represent a client when any one of them practicing alone would be prohibited from doing so" under the provisions regarding conflict of interest, including the one just discussed.[79] Vicarious disqualification based on this rule is not absolute; the affected client may waive disqualification.[80] The corollary rule requires that "when lawyers terminate an association in a firm, none of them, nor any other lawyer with whom any of them subsequently becomes associated, shall knowingly represent a client when doing so involves a material risk of violating" the rules on confidentiality of information or use of information to the disadvantage of a former client.[81] This provision is intended to apply to the members of the law department of a government agency; it is a law firm for purposes of the rule.[82]

Another rule that deals with successive government and private employment with even greater specificity provides:

> (a) Except as law may otherwise expressly permit, a lawyer shall not represent a private client in connection with a matter in which the lawyer participated personally and substantially as a public officer or employee, unless the appropriate government agency consents after consultation. No lawyer in a firm with which that lawyer is associated may undertake or continue representation in the matter unless:
>
> (1) the disqualified lawyer is screened from any participation in the matter and is apportioned no part of the fee therefrom; and

(2) written notice is promptly given to the appropriate government agency to enable it to ascertain compliance with the provisions of this rule.

(b) Except as law may otherwise expressly permit, a lawyer who has knowledge, acquired as a public officer or employee, of confidential government information about a person may not represent a private client whose interests are adverse to that person in a matter in which the information is material. No lawyer in a firm with which that lawyer is associated may undertake or continue representation in the matter unless:

(1) the disqualified lawyer is screened from any participation in the matter and is apportioned no part of the fee therefrom; and

(2) written notice is promptly given to the adverse party to enable that person to ascertain compliance with the provisions of this rule.

(c) Except as law may otherwise expressly permit, a lawyer serving as a public officer or employee shall not:

(1) participate in a matter in which the lawyer participated personally and substantially while in private practice or nongovernmental employment, unless under applicable law no one is, or by lawful delegation may be, authorized to act in the lawyer's stead in the matter; or

(2) negotiate for private employment with any person who is involved as a party or as attorney for a party in a matter in which the lawyer is participating personally and substantially.[83]

The government attorney would be subject to this rule as well as to the rule that precludes representation of adverse interests and the imputed disqualification rules.

Commentary prepared by the drafters of these rules indicates an awareness of the problem of undermining the attractiveness of government service:

> The rules governing lawyers presently or formerly employed by a government agency should not be so restrictive as to inhibit transfer of employment to and from the government. The government has a legitimate need to attract qualified lawyers as well as to maintain high ethical standards. The provisions for screening and waiver are necessary to prevent the disqualification rule from imposing too severe a deterrent against entering public service.[84]

Unquestionably the Kutak Commission rules offer greater precision than the appearance-of-impropriety standard and its progeny of rules. Their explicit recognition of screening—the "Chinese wall"—protects against the perils of literalism under the present Code of Professional Responsibility. The reader is invited to reflect on whether the draft rule is likely to achieve its stated objective of avoiding "too severe a deterrent."

The matter of professional standards is not at all the exclusive province of nationwide organizations. Licensure for the practice of law is a matter primarily within the purview of the states, and national leadership does not ensure local uniformity. For this reason intense debate has occurred in the context of local professional standard setting involving the same matters before the Kutak Commission. Perhaps the most prominent example is found in the efforts of those in the District of Columbia with responsibility for professional standards to deal with the "revolving door."[85] This, of course, comes as no surprise: in what place is it more likely and logical for the former government attorney to ply his trade?

Considerable effort has been and will continue to be devoted to the intricacies of the appropriate ethical standards for the government lawyer, past, present, or prospective. This brief discussion of present and proposed standards should be adequate for its purpose, however, which is to demonstrate that the federal government is not the sole source of ethical constraints that affect the government attorney and that professional standards, as de facto federal law, must be taken into consideration in an assessment of the effects and costs of ethics-in-government laws.

Notes

1. See 18 U.S.C. sec. 201 (1982). There are reasonable and necessary prohibitions concerning the buying of public office, in the form of either nomination or appointment, which naturally apply to activities before one becomes a federal officer or employee (secs. 210–11). Furthermore, most Title 18 prohibitions may affect persons who are in no respects government officers or employees. The one who offers a bribe, for example, is as culpable as the one who accepts.

2. See United States v. Reisley, 35 F. Supp. 102 (D.C.N.J. 1940).

3. See, e.g., United States v. Irwin, 354 F.2d 192 (2d Cir. 1965), cert. denied 383 U.S. 967.

4. See 18 U.S.C. secs. 212–13, 217 (1982).

5. Ibid., secs. 212–13.

6. Ibid., sec. 214.

7. Ibid., secs. 215–17.

8. Ibid., sec. 219.

9. Ibid., sec. 203.

10. Ibid., sec. 205. Neither section 203 nor section 205 applies to retired officers of the uniformed services while not on active duty and not otherwise officers or employees of the United States. See sec. 206.

11. Ibid., sec. 209(a).

12. Ibid., sec. 209(b).

13. Ibid., sec. 209(c).

14. Ibid., sec. 209(e).

15. Ibid., sec. 208(a).

16. Ibid., sec. 208(b).

17. Ibid.

18. Ibid., sec. 207(a).

19. Ibid., sec. 207(b).

20. See ibid., sec. 207(d)(1). This provision provides the basis for determining whether the salary, position, or responsibilities of an officer or employee are of sufficient magnitude to invoke the special provisions for high-level personnel.

21. Ibid., sec. 207(b).

22. Ibid., sec. 207(c).

23. Ibid., sec. 207(d).

24. Ibid., sec. 207(i).

25. Ibid., sec. 207(f).

26. Ibid., sec. 207(h).

27. Ibid., sec. 207(g).

28. Ibid., sec. 218.

29. Ibid., sec. 207(j).

30. 5 U.S.C. secs. 201–11 (App. 1982). The act also contains similar financial disclosure requirements for members of the legislative and judicial branches. See generally 2 U.S.C. secs. 701–9 (Supp. 1982) and 28 U.S.C. secs. 301–9 (Supp. 1982).

31. 5 U.S.C. sec. 201(f) (App. 1982).

32. Ibid., secs. 201(a)–(c).

33. Ibid., sec. 201(d). See also sec. 201(e) concerning filings after termination of government employment.

34. Ibid., sec. 202(a)(1)(A).

35. Ibid., sec. 202(a)(1)(B)(iv).

36. Ibid., sec. 202(a)(2)(A)–(B).

37. Ibid., sec. 202(a)(2)(C).

38. Ibid., sec. 202(a)(3).

39. Ibid., sec. 202(a)(4).

40. Ibid., sec. 202(a)(5).

41. Ibid., sec. 202(a)(6)(A).

42. Ibid., sec. 202(a)(6)(B).

43. Ibid., sec. 202(a)(7).

44. See generally ibid., sec. 202(e).

45. Ibid., sec. 202(f)(1)–(2).

46. Ibid., sec. 202(f)(2)–(3).

47. Ibid., secs. 401–6.

48. Ibid., sec. 202(f)(3)(D).

49. Ibid., sec. 202(f)(5).

50. Ibid., secs. 202(f)(6)(C), 204(a).

51. Ibid., sec. 206.

52. See generally ibid., sec. 205.

53. Ibid., sec. 210.

54. Exec. Order No. 11222, 30 Fed. Reg. 6469 (1965), as amended by Exec. Order No. 11590, 36 Fed. Reg. 7831, reprinted in 18 U.S.C. sec. 201 (1976); 5 C.F.R. sec. 735 (1983).

55. 5 C.F.R. sec. 735.202(a) (1983).

56. Ibid., sec. 735.202(b).

57. Ibid., sec. 735.201(c).

58. Ibid., secs. 735.204–5.

59. Ibid., sec. 735.203.

60. Ibid., sec. 735.207.

61. Ibid., sec. 735.204.

62. Ibid., sec. 735.403.

63. Ibid.

64. Ibid., sec. 735.410.

65. Exec. Order No. 12107, 44 Fed. Reg. 1055 (1978).

66. 5 C.F.R. parts 734–35, 737–38 (1983).

67. 16 C.F.R. part 4.1 (FTC); 32 C.F.R. part 40 (DOD); 41 C.F.R. part 105–735 (GSA); 29 C.F.R. part 2.1–.4 (DOL); 17 C.F.R. part 200, subpart M, .30–14 (SEC); 10 C.F.R. part 1010 (DOE); 7 C.F.R. part 0 (Agriculture).

68. Note, "Developments in the Law—Conflicts of Interest in the Legal Profession," *Harvard Law Review*, vol. 94 (1981), pp. 1244, 1416. This note contains an excellent and extensive discussion of the conflict-of-interest problems government attorneys may confront (pp. 1413–46).

69. ABA Code of Professional Responsibility Canon 9 (1980).

70. Note, "Developments in the Law—Conflicts of Interest in the Legal Profession," *Harvard Law Review*, vol. 94 (1981), pp. 1244, 1415–16.

71. See Bachman v. Pertschuk, 437 F. Supp. 973 (D.C.D.C. 1977).

72. ABA Code of Professional Responsibility D.R. 9-101(B) (1980).

73. Ibid., D.R. 5-105(D).

74. ABA Comm. on Ethics and Professional Responsibility, Formal Opinions, No. 342, p. 2 (1975).

75. Ibid., p. 6.

76. ABA Model Rules of Professional Conduct (Final Draft, August 10, 1982).

77. Ibid., Rule 1.9(a).

78. Ibid., Rule 1.9, Notes.

79. Ibid., Rule 1.10(a).

80. Ibid., Rule 1.10(c).

81. Ibid., Rule 1.10(b).

82. Ibid., Rule 1.10, Comment.

83. Ibid., Rule 1.11.

84. Ibid., Rule 1.11, Comment.

85. See, e.g., D.C. Bar Comm. on Legal Ethics, Opinions, No. 106 (1981).

3
The Effects and Costs of the
Present System

A definitive assessment of the effects and costs of the present system of ethics-in-government laws probably would require the methods of the behavioral sciences and great reliance on empirical research. In this fashion one might attempt to gain an understanding of the motives and considerations that cause persons to enter, remain in, and leave government service. One would hope to probe the minds of as many of these persons as possible—and, at a minimum, of a statistically valid sample. These methods are beyond the reach of this study.

This study draws instead on the assumption—not, perhaps, unduly naive—that persons in or considering government service approach the matter rationally and take the restraints of the ethics-in-government laws into account in making their decisions. This assumption seems reasonable. The ethics-in-government laws are known and knowable; they are neither secret nor particularly arcane. Thus this study relies primarily on the processes of reasoning and prediction in light of the law and common understanding of human nature. In considering the hypothetical case studies presented in this part, the reader is invited to test the validity of the suggested conclusions by asking what effects, if any, the ethics-in-government laws would have on the decisions and actions of a reasonable and reasoning person in such circumstances.

The "Target" Populations and the Question of Differential Effects

Not all government officers and employees are equally affected by the requirements of the ethics-in-government laws, and this fact is not due simply to the probable disposition and inclination of some to run closer to or even beyond the boundaries of lawful conduct. The criminal law provisions of Title 18 apply generally to all in government service. Any employee is a potential object of a bribe

22

and a subsequent criminal action, although clearly the probability that this will occur varies significantly with rank and position. This, of course, is hardly a problem. It is unlikely that foreclosure of opportunities for bribery has ever kept anyone from accepting public employment or led to an early exit; if it has, the government has benefited. Nevertheless, there remains the basic proposition that a law that applies to all does not affect all equally.

There are other examples of this phenomenon in Title 18. It seems improbable that a member of an agency's custodial staff will ever face the "opportunity" of acting as an agent for a foreign principal, but the head of the agency may very well have to face this issue and deal with the prohibition against such representation.[1] Similarly, the provisions dealing with such matters as compensation for services, representation of others in governmental proceedings, personal financial interests, and the permissible activities of former government employees[2] are much less likely to be of concern to the large numbers of persons who perform the necessary yet relatively perfunctory tasks of government.

This is not to suggest that it is undesirable that the provisions of Title 18 will be of little practical concern to a large part of the federal work force. Those who are affected, at least in the sense of keeping an eye to the requirements of the law, are not singled out without reason. Rather they are more often in the higher reaches of government and more likely to hold policy-making positions; consequently, they are more likely to find themselves in situations in which the fact of violations or appearance of conflicts of interest may arise. At these levels of government the reality or appearance of conflicts is much more likely to endanger and undermine public confidence and trust.

The division of the federal work force into two broad segments in relation to the effective workings of the ethics-in-government laws is even more pronounced under the Ethics in Government Act of 1978 and Executive Order No. 11222.[3] The financial disclosure requirements of the act apply only to higher government officers and employees, generally at the level of GS-16 and above.[4] The financial disclosure requirements of the executive order are even more restrictive in application; they reach only agency heads, full-time members of committees, boards, and commissions appointed by the president, and certain other presidential appointees.[5]

Drawing this distinction between those who may be affected by ethics-in-government laws and those who realistically are not puts in perspective the view that a majority of federal employees are not adversely affected by these laws. That may be true, but it is equally true that the majority are not affected at all. The fallacy lies in addressing the population of federal employees as a monolith. Productive analysis is facilitated by differentiation within this population.

Once this initial distinction is made, it is easier to focus on the question of what effect, if any, present ethics-in-government laws are likely to have on decisions to enter, remain in, or leave government service. The proper object for attention, therefore, is persons who are truly affected by these laws, although this study does not extend to elected public officials, who, it may be argued, present different and additional issues in relation to ethics-in-government laws. It is the officer or employee, appointed or hired, in a position subject to the full array of the ethics-in-government laws who is of interest here.

Even within this group there is reason to consider further differentiation to aid analysis. In many respects the group is homogeneous. It is comparatively homogeneous in nature and level of responsibility. Although there are obvious differences between the tasks of the chairman of the Federal Trade Commission and the secretary of the Department of Health and Human Services, both perform high-level policy-making functions and exercise considerable discretion. Their responsibilities are clearly not peripheral, and their roles make them more than supporting cast unless one views all appointed officials as supporting cast for the primary players, the elected officials. Without denigrating the importance of the job of the FTC chairman's personal secretary, it is not difficult to appreciate the difference between him and the chairman.

This group is homogeneous in another important respect: it is homogeneous in opportunity. There is a significant probability that persons in this group have alternatives outside the government, performing similar and even dissimilar tasks. Simply stated, they choose to be in government service. They may be in government for complex and diverse reasons, but few of them are there because there is nowhere else to go. The same is true of those considering government service at such levels. Few are likely to be refugees devoid of choice in the outside world.

It is this relatively homogeneous group that forms the real "target" population for ethics-in-government laws. Its homogeneity is susceptible to overstatement, however. There are differences that may dramatically vary the effect of ethics-in-govenment laws. Limits on outside employment while in government service are irrelevant if there is neither the need nor the inclination to engage in such work. Extensive requirements for disclosure of personal financial

24

worth will not be nettlesome to those with little to disclose. And perhaps only a fortunate few will need to deal with the vagaries of the blind trust. These are but examples, and certainly not surprising ones. Obviously there will be differences that will produce different effects under the ethics-in-government laws, and these should be taken into account as much as possible in assessing the issue that is the object of this study: whether these laws serve as barriers to entry into, exit from, and excellence in the federal public service.

Some Hypothetical Case Studies

The case studies that follow are intended to illustrate and analyze the effects and costs of the present ethics-in-government laws. In an effort to assess those laws and gain some understanding of what, if anything, would cause different persons within the affected "target" population to react differently to their various requirements, the cases are based on varying settings. The principal variables are individual backgrounds, positions, personal financial worth, and career objectives. The case studies do not purport to exhaust all permutations, and no doubt other equally useful possibilities will occur to the reader. The cases have been chosen as representative of the variety of persons who from time to time consider entering or leaving government service and for whom the ethics-in-government laws are at least one factor in their decision.

Each case study is in the form of a first-person narrative of a prospective, present, or past government officer or employee who is sufficiently familiar with the present requirements of the ethics-in-government laws to recognize most potential problems in the process of seeking to take them intelligently into account. Each case is entirely hypothetical. And each is followed by an analytical passage for further development of the legal underpinnings for the officer's or employee's current or anticipated encounter with the ethics-in-government laws. There, as the reader will see, the similarities end.

The Careerist

I am the third son of a former army officer who is now a part-time gentleman farmer in North Carolina. We moved around quite a bit when I was growing up, but home was always the farm in the western part of the state. I was the only one of the four kids who ever showed much taste for chores around the farm. Nobody was surprised when I took my degree in agriculture at State. After the service when

25

the chance came up for a job with Agriculture, I jumped at it.

I've been with the department for twenty-two years now, and I expect to hang in until I retire—I mean really retire. This early retirement business and on to something else isn't for me.

I've been here in Washington for the past fifteen years. My wife and I like this town, and our forty acres in Virginia give me a chance to keep my hand in farming.

USDA's been good to me, and I like to think I've been good for the department. I guess I've been doing something right. The promotions and new responsibilities have come right along every couple of years.

I've seen a lot of folks come and go here—lot of changes, too. Of course, things are a lot more complicated these days than they used to be. I suppose they are all over.

Take this business of ethics in government. Things are a lot tighter there. We have to think about things people didn't pay too much mind to when I joined the department. I think it's a good thing. It can only help, and it sure doesn't hurt. Let me give you a few examples.

There was a time when a bunch of us would go out to dinner after a long day with some of the folks from the other side of the table. When the check came around and they reached for it, nobody from our side fussed too long or too hard. After all, they picked the place, and it wasn't cheap. I never did feel that a free meal affected my work, but those days are gone. Today, anything more than a soft drink or a cup of coffee, unless it's something like dinner at a trade association meeting where you're on the program, and you've got problems.

Of course, there is the paperwork now—the annual ethics reports and things like that. I know that some of our people aren't always happy with what they have to tell the world about. I think it's the publicity that bothers them most. I always tell them they're lucky to have something to fill in. I've never seen a form where I've had to leave so many blanks and almost blanks. But if that's what the government wants, that's what I'll do and gladly. Uncle Sam is my boss and my only boss, the only one I expect I'll ever have.

About my only gripe is that I can't be as active in the Farm Bureau as I'd like. Remember we've got those forty acres in Virginia. But department regulations say no.

The Careerist is probably not atypical—a career government officer or employee, comfortable but not wealthy, who has worked up through an agency's ranks to a position of substantial responsibility, has no reason to treat the position otherwise than as his full-time job, and plans to stay until normal retirement age. By all indications the Careerist is a conscientious public servant whose contributions over the years are substantial and whose longevity in government service lends continuity and stability as administrations and others come and go.

The Careerist, with no plans for outside employment while in government or for other employment after leaving it, is inconvenienced little by the provisions of the ethics-in-government laws and extensive regulations of the Department of Agriculture (USDA) concerning outside employment and conflicts of interest.[6] The problems not eliminated by the boundaries of his plans and ambitions are probably mitigated by his relatively modest personal financial situation.

The farm, if it is a working farm, would appear to constitute outside employment on his own behalf under USDA regulations,[7] but there is no reason to believe that this would be considered an "incompatible activity." An activity would be incompatible if, for example, it resulted in or created the appearance of a conflict of interest, took his time and attention during official working hours, or tended to cause embarrassment to the department. The farm should not fall within any of those categories or any others under the regulations.[8] The regulations aim primarily at outside employment with or for others. Nevertheless, it does appear that operation of even this small farm would require advance approval of the government.[9]

At this stage in his time with USDA, the Careerist is at a level of GS-16 or higher and is therefore subject to the personal financial and other reporting requirements of the Ethics in Government Act.[10] Other persons in USDA are subject to somewhat lesser yet comparable reporting requirements under agency regulations.[11] His situation illustrates the point that if one has relatively little in personal assets, little or nothing in outside income, and a singular commitment to the government job, now and in the future, it is unlikely that the reporting requirements will be viewed as anything but another inconvenient piece of paper. Under these circumstances the philosophy that motivates and underlies the reporting requirements will be readily and, as in the Careerist's case, even cheerfully accepted.

His slightly begrudging acceptance of the policy on the free dinner is perhaps a common attitude. It does seem improbable that an evening on the town at the expense of a person having dealings with an agency is likely to sway a government employee's official judgment, but the law values perceptions as well as the fact of propriety. USDA's regulations on the subject, apparently a product of Executive Order No. 11222 more than of Title 18,[12] are stringent. There is a virtually absolute bar on the solicitation or acceptance of gifts, entertainment, or any other thing of monetary value, including complimentary meals and beverages, from persons regulated by or dealing with the department. Among the few permissible exceptions are the soft drink and cup of coffee to which the Careerist referred, and even these may be accepted only if "wholly free of any embarrassing or improper implications."[13]

Indeed, the Careerist's complaints and reservations concerning the application of the ethics-in-government laws to him are minuscule in comparison with their potential reach. His only complaint of any intensity concerns the limitation that USDA regulations place on his activities with the American Farm Bureau Federation. His membership in this or other farm organizations is not prohibited, but he may not participate in certain activities, such as the recruitment of members.[14] At the same time it is likely that the Careerist would accept the legitimacy of the policy on which the regulation is founded, that the department "shall deal fairly with all organizations and deal with each upon the same basis."[15]

A fair and reasonable conclusion is that present ethics-in-government laws would not have been sufficient to persuade him not to join the government and, once he was in, would certainly not have contributed to a premature departure. Admittedly these laws have an effect on the Careerist, but their cost to him is negligible. The government in this case is not likely to be deprived of a dedicated and valued employee in the name of ethics in government.

The Industrialist

Last week an acquaintance of mine who is now with the government called to ask what I would think about being appointed to a high post in the Defense Department. My initial reaction, quite honestly, was, Why me? I really have no experience in the field. I've been with my company for thirty-five years, and we always have been and probably always will be in consumer products. He said what they needed was good people with management skills no matter what their area. My friend asked me to think about it— nothing formal at this point—and I said I was flattered and would at least do that.

I must admit that the chance to go to Washington is intriguing. I'm sure that my wife and I would enjoy the challenge. But the big question is whether I would want to leave a job I love and like to think I do quite well. The truth is it really would be a decision to retire from the company. By the time I'd expect to complete my stint at Defense (my friend told me not to plan on more than two years because even the president's contract is up for renewal then), I'd be less than a year away from retirement anyway. But I suppose I could take a leave of absence for now rather than early retirement.

I guess my biggest question concerns finances. It's not the government salary, although this would be the first new title I ever picked up at a quarter of my old salary. What does concern me is the effect the new job would have on my estate. My wife and I started with nothing and now, I'm not ashamed to say, have quite a lot. We've worked hard and made some pretty solid investments. The best of all has been the stock I've acquired in the company through options. Today it's worth well over a million dollars.

The reason my estate comes to mind is that after my friend called I was thinking about my comment that I really didn't know anything about the Defense Department. That's true, but the company did do over $200 million worth of business with the department last year. Soldiers are consumers too. It would be one thing to part with the company, but I refuse to part with my stock. That's one we'll have to explore.

Actually, there is no way I could cut my ties with the company even if I did take early retirement to go to Washington. There would still be payments under the pension plan and the deferred compensation plan for officers and directors. Oh, perhaps I could renounce my interest in them, but seriously . . .

Anyway, my hope would always be to be with the company as long as they wanted me. Maybe I would have to resign my seat on the board if I went with Defense, but my secret hope would be that when I finished there would still be a place for me on the board.

Well, they talk about "food for thought." I guess I've got plenty.

Although some might disagree vehemently, most persons would probably recognize the attractiveness to the government of obtaining the services of a proven and experienced executive such as the Industrialist. As a high-ranking official in a Fortune 500 company, he has acquired the managerial skills necessary to the successful operation of a large, complex, and intrinsically bureaucratic organization not unlike the Defense Department, though on a relatively smaller scale. Consequently, it is not overstatement to suggest that the government might benefit if he were to join it even for as short a time as two years.

In this instance the government's task is to persuade as well as to extend an offer. Acceptance will not result in direct, personal economic gain; the salary is at best a neutral element in the Industrialist's decision. The ethics-in-government laws raise additional considerations, which from a strictly personal point of view may be negative. Of course, they are negative only with respect to the government's desire to obtain his services. They may be salutary and beneficial as reflections of other and perhaps higher values. But the Industrialist should not be accused of undue selfishness or an absence of values because of his concern for the personal implications of a decision to join Defense. As is most often the case in these situations, the government placed the call.

In assessing the relationship between an appointment in the Department of Defense and his personal affairs and perhaps post-government employment, the Industrialist must take into account not only Title 18, the Ethics in Government Act, and Executive Order No. 11222 but also Defense Department regulations.[16]

At the moment the Industrialist is not affected by the ethics-in-government laws. He has not yet been appointed or even informed of his impending appointment.[17] All he is doing now is thinking about the possibilities, and, as he suspects, there is much to think about.

The principal issues of concern to him involve matters of personal finance arising out of his relationship with his present employer. The Industrialist could sever all direct ties with the company in a traditional sense and still have connections with it. The most prominent of these would be the continued ownership of substantial stockholdings in the company, but the pension and deferred compensation payments would also fall in this class. His situation is complicated by the fact that the company does have substantial sales to the Defense Department, which are likely to continue.

The department has stated by regulation that "government employment, as a public trust, requires that . . . personnel place loyalty to country, ethical principles, and law above private gain and other interests."[18] This statement is given more definitive meaning pertinent to the Industrialist in other regulations.

One provides that Defense Department personnel are not to "engage in any personal, business or professional activity, or receive or retain any direct or indirect financial interest, which places them in a position of conflict between their private interests and the public interests of the United States related to the duties or responsibilities of their DOD positions."[19] Ownership of stock in the company or continuation on the board could conflict with this requirement. The regulation is not as unequivocal as it first appears, however. Another regulation provides that as a general matter personnel with affiliations or financial interests that create conflicts or appearances of conflicts with their official duties must disqualify themselves from the duties affected. If a person disqualifies himself in accordance with this rule and, as a consequence, finds that he is not able to perform his duties adequately, he must do one of two things: divest himself of the interest and terminate the affiliation or be removed from that position in the department.[20] Thus the prohibition is not absolute; but given the alternatives if disqualification is required, it is not very far removed.

That the Industrialist's stockholdings are small in relation to the total outstanding shares of the company and that the company's sales to the department are minuscule in relation to its total purchases are not especially relevant. It is the existence of a relationship between private interest and public duty that is determinative. Another regulation illustrates further the Industrialist's potential dilemma. It does exempt certain shareholdings from the disqualification requirements, but the exception applies only to holdings in "widely held, diversified" mutual funds or regulated investment companies on the ground that these holdings are "too remote or inconsequential to affect the services of Government personnel."[21]

The key for the Industrialist will be the nature of his anticipated duties in the department. His position may involve responsibilities without even the remotest relationship to the interests of the company. If so, he may be able to retain his shares. Yet he has been recruited for a position of more than minor significance, and the higher he goes in the department, the wider the range of his duties is likely to be and the greater the probability of at least the appearance of a conflict. Similar considerations, as well as the department's prohibition of outside employment "incompatible" with an individual's duties,[22] would apply to continuation on the company's board of directors.

What the Industrialist may discover he must seriously consider is a blind trust for his financial interests, including his stock in the company. It seems clear that he would prefer this to divestiture. A trust, however, would probably give him special cause for concern and might not satisfy his personal goals.

As the regulations promulgated under the Ethics in Government Act indicate, the blind trust may mute the effects of conflicts of

31

interests and reduce or eliminate the need for divestiture of personal financial interests.

> Prior to enactment of the Act's qualified trust provisions, there was no accepted trust definition of a properly formulated blind trust. However, there was general agreement that the use of blind trusts frequently could ameliorate potential conflict of interest situations. An underlying concept is that if a Government official does not know the identity of his or her financial interests, his or her official actions should not be subject to collateral attack by questions of the appearance of such a conflict. In other words, if the Government official does not know what he or she owns, it is impossible for him or her intentionally to take actions to benefit specifically his or her own personal interests. Therefore, the general public policy goal to be achieved through the use of blind trusts is an actual "blindness" or lack of knowledge by the Government official with respect to the holdings held in trust.[23]

The difficulty is that a trust will be considered blind only with respect to assets acquired by an independent trustee after its creation; any asset initially placed in the trust will be considered an asset of the government official for purposes of federal conflict-of-interest laws.[24] Thus the Industrialist's potential problems would continue as long as he insisted on retaining his shares in the company, even if he were to create a qualified diversified trust to contain a well-diversified portfolio of readily marketable securities.[25] Since the Industrialist's portfolio is not now diversified, the independent trustee under a diversified trust would certainly have to sell some and perhaps all of his holdings in the company. At this juncture tax considerations also may be of more than passing interest even if he has found other reasons to accept parting with his shares.

The outlook seems brighter concerning his pension and deferred compensation. At least with regard to the prohibition of the receipt of salary or other compensation from any source other than the United States, an exception is made for continued participation "in a bona fide pension, retirement, group life, health or accidental insurance, profit-sharing, stock bonus, or other employee welfare or benefit plan maintained by a former employer."[26] Nevertheless, these payments would require further analysis in light of the Industrialist's actual government duties, the terms of the plans, and other elements of the ethics-in-government laws.

Furthermore, there is the question of postemployment conflicts of interest. At this point it is difficult to assess just what the precise limitations on the Industrialist might be, because of uncertainty about what his and the company's activities will be in the ensuing years. The probability is great, however, that there will be some effect, though not as great as in some of the case studies that follow, in which the individuals have longer and more ambitious plans for the future.

However he resolves the matters of personal finance, the Industrialist will be at a level that will require financial reports under the Ethics in Government Act and Department of Defense regulations if he decides to join the department.[27] There is nothing to suggest that he is especially troubled by this prospect, but whether the other issues can be resolved to his satisfaction is highly questionable.

The "Middle" Manager

I've been in local politics since I was in high school. I've never run for office or anything like that, but I've spent some time helping several people who made it. I make my living in the industrial relations department of one of the country's largest companies and have been with them for over ten years and really like it.

But last week was some week. I got a call from a man at the Department of Labor who said he had heard about me from one of my old candidates who had moved on and up. He said he wanted me to think seriously about coming to work for him in the department and that, if I was interested, he'd like to get together to talk about it. I told him I would talk to my boss and my wife and kids and get back to him.

I'm really excited about the opportunity. The work I would do ties in nicely with the labor-management relations work I've been doing the past few years. I've got some ideas I'd like to try out, and this job would be high enough up to give me a chance. The nice thing is that it's not so high that I'd need to worry about nosebleeds.

I talked with my boss. He was as excited about it as I was, I think. He said that he was pretty sure that the company would go along with a leave of absence, if I wanted. That sounds just right to me. He even said he had some ideas for how my experience in the department would move me along when I returned.

Things were a lot more complicated at home. Everybody seemed to like the idea, but when we sat down with the budget, the numbers were a nightmare. I've been with the company long enough and moved up nicely enough to be doing pretty well. Anyway, the Labor position would pay about twelve-five less than I make now. From what we hear about the cost of living in Washington, we just don't see how we could make it. That would seem crazy to our folks with the money I make now, but it's true. My wife suggested that since I would be coming back, maybe the company could help out. That's first on my list when I get into the office tomorrow. There better be something. Otherwise, forget it.

This is a classic case of a "revolving door" that is virtually assured of eventually running full circle. The Middle Manager is of an age and inclination that make his return to the private sector from government service predictable. His case is also classic in that it reflects what is uniquely a middle-class problem. He is sufficiently well off financially that acceptance of the government position would be a professional step forward, as he sees it, and a personal step backward. But he is not so well off that he is able to do anything about it. Although his immediate concern is the adequacy of government compensation, the ethics-in-government laws compound the problem. They are part of the environment in which the adequacy or inadequacy of compensation is determined and thus may contribute to depriving the government of the services of otherwise valuable persons.

The reality is that the Middle Manager must accept a substantial reduction in salary if he joins the Labor Department. Unlike the Industrialist, who would take an even greater salary reduction in going to the Department of Defense, the Middle Manager does not have the personal financial resources to cushion the loss of $12,500 in income. Some may join the government with an increase in income, and others such as the Industrialist and the Middle Manager may join it and experience a reduction. But of all these it is the Middle Manager who suffers most demonstrably. There is, for most persons, an abstract quality to the Industrialist's concern about his large stockholdings. There is nothing abstract in the situation the Middle Manager confronts. He must decide not simply whether he is willing but whether he is able to join the government. It is also different for someone who has considerably less than the Middle Manager and will realize an increase in income in accepting a government position. It is the increase or decrease and not the actual compensation that is important.

The Middle Manager's difficulty is aggravated by his inability to turn elsewhere for assistance. He cannot turn to personal resources, which he does not have. His spouse might move into the job market, if that additional resource has not already been tapped. He might consider supplementing his government income through outside employment. His prospective superior, however, might be expected to look askance at this; he may view the government position as more than a full-time job in itself. Even with his superior's consent, the Middle Manager would be limited in his choice of outside employment by availability and the ethics-in-government laws. Although he would not be subject to the 15 percent limit for presidential appointees who must be confirmed by the Senate,[28] he would be precluded from outside employment that resulted in real or apparent conflict of interest.[29] Since his best opportunities are likely to involve the very areas of expertise that make him attractive to the government, outside employment within his competence may be difficult to find. The only work within his field that is likely to be allowed is teaching, lecturing, or writing.[30] The reader can reach his or her own judgment on the likelihood of the Middle Manager's finding such work and filling the $12,500 gap.

The only other realistic alternative, in the absence of a rich uncle, is his present employer, to whom he expects to return after leaving the government. A simple solution to his problem would be to have his present employer supplement his income while he is in the government by an amount at least sufficient to permit the move without any loss. Even if his employer were favorably inclined, the basic principle of "one master" under the ethics-in-government laws presents serious obstacles.

One of the provisions of Title 18 is relevant to the question. The receipt or payment of "any salary, or any contribution to or supplementation of salary, as compensation for . . . services as an officer or employee"[31] is generally prohibited. This is exactly what the Middle Manager appears to have in mind and precisely what he needs. But the statute precludes it. The statute was amended in 1979 to accommodate certain payments in connection with executive exchange and fellowship programs to make clear the status of payments of relocation expenses. Under the amendment such payments are permissible, without regard to the general prohibition, for such programs created by statute or executive order for appointments of one year or less.[32] But this exception will not solve the Middle Manager's problem. The objective of uniformity of pay for like government services is preserved by the general prohibition; uniformity of effect is another matter.

There are other exceptions. One would protect the Middle Manager's employee benefits, which might carry over.[33] This is sensible because such benefits are really compensation for past service rather than for government service. An even more striking possibility is the exception if the officer or employee serves without compensation entirely.[34] This is where the rich uncle comes into play, and it seems that the entire sojourn in Washington could be underwritten by the firm if it wanted to do so; but that is asking what is not likely to be forthcoming in most cases, including the Middle Manager's. What his employer had in mind when he spoke of a leave of absence was probably an unpaid leave with the promise of employment upon return. To expect the company to do more, if it were possible, than provide a modest supplement is to expect the unreasonable. Perhaps the Middle Manager must await the day when scholarships are awarded in connection with government service; but should that day arrive, he would no doubt fail to satisfy the applicable standard of need.

The other principal issue that should be of concern involves the limits that may be placed on his activities on the company's behalf when he returns from the department. At this point that is difficult to determine because the duties of his government job are known only in general terms and even less is known about his company position in the future. The possibility of postemployment conflict of interest does exist in that his present job, his government job, and his subsequent company job will probably have labor relations matters in common. It is known that he will not be allowed to switch to the company's side in matters involving the company in which he participated personally and substantially while in the government.[35] This should not present a significant problem, since he probably should be disqualified in such cases while in the government.[36] Furthermore, department regulations would preclude representation of the company in any case or administrative proceeding pending during the time of his employment, unless written consent were obtained from the department.[37] All these issues, however, will require more definitive resolution in the future. The Middle Manager must be aware that they will arise, but none appear to be of sufficient magnitude to cause him to decline the invitation. Adequate compensation remains the determining consideration in his decision.

What the Middle Manager will do is uncertain. The probable outcome, however, is that he will express his appreciation and his regrets. The compensation is inadequate for him, even if not for others, and the ethics-in-government laws preclude any practical solution to meet his needs.

The Entrepreneur

Several years after I graduated from college, my old roommate and I did what we had talked about doing when we were in school. We started our own business. Both of us had some exposure to computers in school but learned our way around later in business. We saw things starting to move in a direction we felt we could handle on our own and took off.

At first it was your classic shoestring operation, but our specialty is software—computer programs, you know—and we were fortunate and first with some ideas that took off. Today it's hard to believe. Here I am, just turned thirty-three and a millionaire several times over. My partner and I own Computech entirely, fifty-fifty, and it's fun.

Now, all of a sudden, life is getting complicated. This fellow from Washington called me last week and asked if I'd like to spend a couple of years in the international trade area in the Commerce Department. Since I handle most of the marketing for our company, they thought I might be an asset in establishing trade policy for computer technology. I think they like my age, too—must be some kind of youth kick.

It all sounds pretty good. We're not so small anymore, and my partner said he could hold down the fort if I wanted to go for a few years. The only hitch might be one the guy who called mentioned. He said that there might be a problem with the 50 percent I own of Computech stock. We'll have to work on that one. Conservatively I think my share is worth about eight million. I want to keep it. In fact, I'm going to. If the problem is that the work I would do in Commerce involves computers, there may be no way out. That's the only thing I know. It's not as if I could help them worry about auto imports.

By most standards the Entrepreneur is entitled to congratulations and best wishes for continued success. At an early age he has created a new and substantial enterprise in a field of emerging technology. He and his partner have achieved this in the best traditions of American capitalism. With little to begin with, they have created much in response to new needs and demands in the marketplace. And there is no reason to believe that they are finished. Now the Entrepreneur has attracted an invitation for public service to give broader application to his skills and expertise.

The ethics-in-government laws are likely to dampen the Entrepreneur's enthusiasm for the prospect of the position at the Commerce Department because of the relationship between his business interests and the proposed field of his government activities. That both involve computers makes it probable that real and apparent conflicts of interest will arise, and the fact that his knowledge and experience in computers are what attracted the government in the first place is irrelevant. The most obvious and unacceptable solution to the problem would be total separation from the company, including divestiture of his 50 percent shareholdings. This solution is unacceptable to all concerned because it is unacceptable to the Entrepreneur. The question remains whether anything can be done to preserve his utility to the government and his interests in the company.

One possibility is to structure the activities of the company and the duties and responsibilities at Commerce so as to reduce the potential for conflict. If the company stays out of certain kinds of business and the Entrepreneur avoids certain activities, there may be only limited conflicts of interest or none. It is doubtful, however, that the other shareholder will especially like that idea. It is one thing to agree to hold the fort in the Entrepreneur's absence, as he did, and quite another to agree to dismantle part of the enterprise or not add to it in the future; but any extensive curtailment of the Entrepreneur's duties at Commerce would deprive the government of the fullest benefit from his services.

Another possibility would be to deal with the issues as they arise in light of his precise duties and the company's activities at any particular time. If they took this course, both would find it imperative to proceed with a constant eye to the Title 18 provision concerning official acts affecting a personal financial interest. Personal and substantial participation by the Entrepreneur in any "decision, approval, disapproval, recommendation, the rendering of advice, investigation, or otherwise, in a . . . proceeding, application, request for a ruling, or other determination, contract, claim, controversy, . . . or other particular matter in which, to his knowledge, he, his spouse, minor child, partner, organization in which he is serving as officer, [or] director . . . has a financial interest" would be prohibited.[38] There is, however, a possibility of relief from this provision. If the department is informed in advance of the potential transgression, it may make a written determination that the financial "interest is not so substantial as to be deemed likely to affect the integrity of the services which the Government may expect."[39] Understandably this is a potentially burdensome and unpredictable means of relief. Again, the simple and unacceptable answer is to eliminate the conflict by eliminating the interest.

There are other alternatives to be considered, but these too are not without difficulty. Assuming the Entrepreneur were willing to abandon all direct executive connections with the company, including positions as an officer and a director, the shareholdings must be considered. As a direct financial interest, his shares are a sufficient nexus to perpetuate the conflict-of-interest issues. The difficulty is aggravated in this case by the closely held nature of the company. As a voting shareholder of 50 percent of the shares, the Entrepreneur would continue to be in shared control with his "partner." To remove even the appearance of control would require some alteration in his relationship to the shares.

One possibility the ethics-in-government laws hold out is the qualified trust, the purpose of which is to insulate the officer or employee from his financial holdings in a manner that will eliminate conflicts of interest.[40] But the trust is not an effective shield with respect to assets initially placed in trust. "The trust is considered blind only as to assets subsequently purchased by the trustee."[41] And by definition the qualified diversified trust is of no use to the Entrepreneur. He has no desire for the kind of diversity that the law envisions.

In this instance, therefore, it is reasonable to conclude that there is no practicable way by which the occasional fact and frequent appearance of conflict between his personal interests and the interests of the government can be addressed. Since he is not willing to sell his interest in the company—a reasonable position in light of his expectation of returning—he should not accept the offer of this particular job. One may become available later for which he is fully unqualified and entirely acceptable—an ambassadorship perhaps.

Considering the magnitude of the obstacles to entry, only brief mention is necessary of the issues the Entrepreneur would face upon leaving the government. He would have to consider the limits on postemployment activities, such as, for example, the ban on switching sides in matters in which he had been actively involved in government.[42] If he were a senior employee, there would be other limitations to consider.[43] It is unfortunate for the government, since it pursued the services of the Entrepreneur, that only the remotest course of events will provide an opportunity to wrestle with these postemployment issues.

The Heir

I can only characterize myself as fortunate, and my hope and expectation is that I will always be able to carry that special responsibility well.

Shortly before the turn of the century a quite remarkable man, my great-grandfather, established himself as one of the dominant figures of his generation and one of the creators of the industrial base of America. I would not necessarily say that I condone all the methods he employed in building his empire, but I imagine they were not inconsistent with the temper of his times. In any event, it was the efforts of this man that permit me to call myself fortunate.

The fortune that great-grandfather founded has been preserved and passed down to later generations in our family, including my own. I hope you won't take me as overbearing if I say that this has passed on to our family both responsibilities and opportunities. One of the responsibilities to which all members of the family have been committed—though, I must admit, with varying fervor—is service to the public.

So when the president appointed me to the commission a few years ago, there was no uncertainty in my mind. Indeed, I viewed the move as a natural extension to a different sphere of the philanthropic activities in which I was engaged at the time.

The move to Washington was a delightful homecoming of sorts. We lived here for several years when I was a child while my father was deputy assistant secretary of state.

But back to the reason I consider myself fortunate: great-grandfather placed the assets of his estate in a trust. The trust was large then and is significantly larger today. I hope you won't be embarrassed if I say so, but the trust brings me over half a million dollars a year in income. You can now appreciate my point.

As you know, the business is as dominant a force as ever in the economy. However, it has been years since anyone in our family has been actively involved. Actually, shares in the business were once the principal trust asset, but the bank that serves as trustee diversified the portfolio long ago. The last report I saw showed that less than 5 percent of the assets were in shares in great-grandfather's company.

When I joined the government, some adjustments were made in the trust to satisfy the ethics laws, and now I am very much insulated from the activities of the trustee, with the exception of the fortunate aspects. I also have a trust for my personal assets, which I am equally divorced from.

As for the future, some of the people at home have apparently been impressed with my performance with the commission and are urging me to run for the Senate. Of course, I'm flattered, as anyone would be, and I'm going to give the prospect serious thought.

As the Heir and most others would readily concede, he is indeed fortunate, and although great wealth no doubt has its burdens, the reach of his good fortune extends to matters of ethics in government. Furthermore, at least in this instance, "old" money has considerable advantages over "new."

The Heir's transition to public life was relatively untroubled. Apparently he had been a generalist engaged in various philanthropic activities. He was not about the business of building his fortune; it had been made and passed on some time before. Consequently, the Heir did not arrive in Washington with the more obvious potential conflicts of the Industrialist, the Middle Manager, and the Entrepreneur, whose personal finances and expertise were in varying but much greater degree intertwined.

The Heir's principal difficulty upon joining the government was the necessity of insulation from his personal fortune and from his interest in the trust created by his great-grandfather. In the case of the trust and apparently his personal assets, he was aided significantly by a situation for which no one would have planned in anticipation of his joining the government: both were well diversified.

Although it is not clear from what he said about his trusts, it seems that prudence, if not actuality, suggested that he could avoid the fact or appearance of conflict with his duties at the commission by creating a qualified blind trust or a diversified trust for his personal assets and reaching a suitable agreement with the trustee under the family trust to insulate him sufficiently from information concerning its activities to satisfy the requirements of the Ethics in Government Act.[44]

In addition to any other income, his receipts from these trusts are, of course, subject to the executive personnel financial disclosure requirements under the act.[45] Information about the value of his assets must also be reported.[46] It would not be unexpected if the publicity that attends the requisite financial disclosure were to trouble the Heir, but he has given no indication that it does and seems comfortable with his present circumstances. Nonetheless, if he decides to seek elected office, the public nature of the information, together with the personal assets and political strategy of his opposition, may cause him to reconsider.

Whether or not he becomes a senator awaits his own and the voters' decision. If he does, he will not have the same concerns as he would in returning to private life. To remain in government in an elected capacity is to remain subject to the ethics-in-government laws but not to their postemployment aspects. The issue of the "revolving door" lies somewhere in the future, if anywhere, for the Heir.

The Professor

Two years ago I took a leave of absence from my faculty position at State to join the Environmental Protection Agency. I had worked with EPA under a grant several years before, and when they set up an internal task force of scientists to study toxic wastes, they called me.

My department chairperson at State agreed that it was a superb professional opportunity and saw to the details of the leave. University policy prohibits leaves of more than three years, and next semester we will be returning. The most exciting thing is that I have been named university vice president for scientific affairs. I'll miss the classroom and the laboratory, but it seemed about time to try my hand at administration.

The work at EPA has been rewarding. Don't confuse that with finances. Actually the pay here has been about what it was at State. That surprised me, but next year will be a bit better. At EPA I put in twelve or more hours a day. My family saw Washington, but I'm afraid I didn't see too much.

One thing that surprised me was that I was subject to the ethics act. I filled out my forms each year. They weren't much trouble. We've saved some, but all of it is in CDs at the bank. Nothing exotic about our family, or so my son tells me. I didn't think my job there would be high enough for that, but I guess it was.

Before I leave, the one thing I really have to investigate is what effect this job might have on my new one. I heard recently that a woman in another agency who left for an administrative position at a private university out West had some trouble in reconciling the two after she left.

The Professor's transition from the academic community to government appears to have been smooth so far as the ethics-in-government laws are concerned. There is no indication that he had engaged in activities, such as private consulting in his specialty, that could have raised issues of conflicts of interest at EPA. His personal finances were and remain uncomplicated by investments such as stockholdings, which could have the same effect. His earlier work on a government grant, perhaps as a special government employee,[47] appears to have been his only prior nonuniversity employment. His was an easy and uneventful entry in terms of the ethics-in-government laws.

The Professor's time at EPA was similarly untroubled in this respect. He appears to have been more than a full-time employee, devoting long hours to the job. He was neither inclined nor compelled to seek outside employment, and his uncomplicated personal finances made compliance with the executive financial reporting requirements under the act a fairly routine matter.

The Professor's postemployment position in relation to conflicts of interest, however, may present him with some surprises. Universities "do business" with the government. An array of grants and subsidies make up a substantial part of the resources of almost all institutions of higher education. The outcries against current retrenchment in this support are evidence of its importance to them. Furthermore, the Professor is not simply returning to the state university as a teacher and researcher; he is returning as a high administrative official with responsibilities likely to include matters of federal support of the university's scientific research. This is sufficient reason for a closer examination of the effect of the ethics-in-government laws on his situation.

The Professor may well discover that he confronts many of the issues that would face the Industrialist, the Middle Manager, and the Entrepreneur. Since he is leaving federal employment to go to an institution that has numerous dealings with the government, the potential for conflicts does exist, especially in light of his new responsibilities at the university, which will include supervision of its research establishment. Research at such institutions customarily means work for, support from, and contacts with the federal government, and in his case EPA may be expected to be on the list.

Despite the similarities, the Professor's position with respect to EPA once he leaves will be less restricted than it would be if he were to join a different kind of organization in the private sector. This is because the ethics-in-government laws on occasion reflect a solicitous attitude toward certain kinds of postgovernment employment, including positions with educational institutions.

Actually this distinction may be seen in the law with respect to certain employees before their departure from government. The general prohibition of compensation or salary supplements from sources other than the United States does not apply to contributions from the treasury of a state, county, or municipality.[48] If the Professor had taken a sabbatical leave for a year at half pay, the argument might be made that this supplement to his federal salary was not barred because the state was its source. The argument is plausible because of the statutory exemption. It would not be available if the Professor held a comparable position at a private university and received pay from the school while on sabbatical and in government service. This illustrates the distinction sometimes made under the ethics-in-government laws.

The Professor will find similar and more directly relevant distinctions after leaving and assuming his new post. In general he may not represent the university by formal or informal appearances, or oral or written communications, in particular matters in which he participated at EPA.[49] If, however, he participated in the development of, for example, a general policy on toxic waste research for EPA, he could represent the university in seeking a grant under the program that eventually developed.[50] The difference lies in the particular as opposed to the general.

The same prohibition would extend to any matters that had been pending under his responsibility during his EPA years, though only for two years after termination of his employment.[51] Under another provision the Professor, as a senior employee at EPA, would also be barred for two years from lending his personal presence to informal or formal appearances of another before the agency in matters in which he participated personally and substantially.[52]

Yet another provision generally precludes for a period of one year a senior employee's direct representation of another person with the former agency in any matter pending before the agency in which the agency has a direct and substantial interest.[53] Prior involvement by the former employee is not required under this provision; in fact, it applies to matters that arise during the year after the employee leaves.[54] This requirement in particular might be of great interest to the Professor if the university expects any significant dealings with EPA in the coming year. But the statute draws a distinction useful to the Professor. This limitation does not apply to, among others, persons whose principal occupation or employment is with an accredited, degree-granting institution of higher education.[55]

Moreover, communications solely for the purposes of providing EPA with scientific or technological information are not barred, notwithstanding the other provisions of the law and the former employee's participation or responsibility in any matter.[56] Further, the administrator of EPA could certify that the scientific or technical expertise of a former employee was necessary to the agency and in the national interest and thus justify exemption of the former employee from the otherwise applicable provisions of the law.[57]

As this discussion suggests, the Professor will discover that he must devote more attention to ethics in government once he leaves government service than he did while he was in it. He should also find that none of the relevant legal requirements place insurmountable obstacles before him in discharging his new responsibilities for the university and that most of the restrictions on his activities with EPA will disappear in a year or two at most.

The Lawyer

When I got out of law school, I took the bar exam and a long vacation and joined the department. I've been here for seven years, but as I expected when I started, there comes a time when you should move on. I'm not entirely happy with the policies my new boss has implemented. This isn't entirely new because I've had lots of bosses in the last seven years. They've come and gone, but I guess I'm not as flexible as I used to be.

I've had a wide range of experience in the department and in the past few years some major responsibility. Whether as an active participant or as an adviser, I think I've been involved in every important legal proceeding in the department lately, ranging from rulemaking to formal adjudication.

Last week I sent out résumés to a number of private firms. Considering the number of years I have been out, an important consideration for me is just where I would fit in at a firm. I realize that it is asking a lot of some firms, but I think that my experience should allow me to move into a firm at the partner level. I don't think I should have to serve a few years' apprenticeship as an associate. We'll see.

Actually the best opportunity for me would be with a firm I have dealt with several times in recent years. Once in a case I got them good, and instead of being mad, one of the senior partners told me that if I ever decided to leave, I should let them know. I think my chances with them might be pretty good.

What troubles me is the conflict-of-interest business. It's not in anyone's interest for me to work on anything where there is even the slightest appearance of impropriety. I'm not talking about what the law and the bar standards are. I have no interest in going as far as the law allows. My personal standards, I like to think, are higher than that.

Of course, the best thing for me to do would be to drop out for a year or two and then come back all nice and clean. The problem is that I can't afford to do that. Maybe I haven't saved as much as I should have, but the truth is that I need that regular paycheck to live on. The other alternative, at least for a time, would be to practice in an area having nothing to do with the department. That has it problems, too. I'm afraid all I could expect would be a neophyte's wages for a neophyte's work.

Well, I'll see what the letters look like when they come in.

It appears that the Lawyer has been an effective and conscientious government attorney. She is not atypical in her decision not to make government legal service a lifetime commitment but to move on within the profession in the private sector. She is also hardly unusual in her need for a continuing source of livelihood. Her high personal standards may be equally common, and there is no reason to believe they are not.

The Lawyer's life in the law of conflicts of interest appears to have been uncomplicted thus far. That is about to change. One reason for this is the prevalence of specialization in the legal profession. This is perhaps nowhere more evident than among government agencies. The division of tasks among myriad agencies that are themselves specialists virtually ensures that most government attorneys are expert in relatively narrow areas of the law. This degree of specialization is often mirrored among members of the private bar with whom the government attorney deals, and it is this group of private specialists that, through familiarity and inclination, is most likely to provide a market for the government attorney's services. These are the persons who will find the government attorney's expertise and specialization useful and attractive. As a result the attorneys to whom the Lawyer is most inclined to turn for private employment are the ones with whom she is most likely to encounter issues of conflict of interest.

As a first step the Lawyer should determine whether any of the law firms to whom she has written have any matters pending before the department in which she is participating personally and substantially. Title 18 prohibits such relationships between a government employee and "any person or organization with whom he is negotiating or has any arrangement concerning prospective employment"[58] to the extent that the employee has knowledge. It would be surprising if there were not some in this category among those to whom she sent résumés. If there are, however, there is a possibility of relief. If she obtains in advance a written determination from her superiors that the potentially conflicting interests are not so substantial "as to be deemed likely to affect the integrity of the services which the Government may expect from"[59] her, there is no potential violation of this provision concerning acts affecting a personal financial interest.

Beyond this issue are others that may affect her ability to obtain a new position of her choice and to her liking. The Lawyer must consider what limits there would be on her activities when she becomes a former government attorney in private practice. This will be of more than passing interest to prospective colleagues, who will also be interested in whether any disqualification that applies to her would apply vicariously to them. This issue introduces an interesting dimension into negotiations for future employment: must we restrict our activities because you must restrict yours?

As one could anticipate, she could not represent a client in her new position in a matter in which she was personally and substantially involved on behalf of the government. This variety of switching sides is prohibited.[60] To determine this and other conflicts-of-interest issues, she would find it necessary to review her own activities and those of her prospective employer thoroughly. Apparently she had reached a position of some responsibility in the department and may find that substantial and personal participation includes a greater number of matters than might normally be expected. There may even be matters with which she was less closely connected that fall within a two-year statutory restriction because they were pending within the year before she left and under her responsibility.[61]

It is not certain whether the Lawyer is a senior employee for purposes of the restrictions on former government employees. If she is, there would be even more restrictions to consider, such as the limits on certain personal appearances for a year or two.[62]

The question of vicarious disqualification is more difficult. Title 18 provides that the partner of an officer or employee may not act as agent or attorney in matters in which the United States is a party or has a direct or substantial interest if the officer or employee is participating or has participated in the matter in a personal and substantial way.[63] This provision, however, does not address disqualification of partners of officers and employees after they have left office. The regulations on postemployment conflicts of interest note that "neither the Act nor these regulations impute the restrictions on former employees to partners or associates of such employees."[64] For most former employees this means that the question of vicarious disqualification disappears, but this is not the case for the Lawyer.

Unlike others, an attorney must consider the pronouncements of the professional associations and the courts on the subject of vicarious disqualification. Activities fully consistent with federal statutes and regulations may be contrary to professional standards. Actually, this dichotomy is possible with respect to the other requirements applicable to the former government attorney. The government's regulations provide the following illustration.

A senior Justice Department lawyer personally works on an antitrust case against Z Company. After leaving the Department, she is asked to discuss legal strategy with lawyers representing Z Company on the same antitrust case, to write portions of the brief and to direct the research of the staff working on the case. Any such aid would not be prohibited by the statute, but would likely be prohibited by professional disciplinary rules.[65]

Although the result reached under the professional standards may well be the correct one, the divergence between federal law and professional standards is striking and demonstrates how the standards have become de facto federal law on vicarious disqualification for former government attorneys and their colleagues.

As a member of the District of Columbia Bar seeking employment with a firm in the District, the Lawyer and her future employer are subject to the disciplinary rules of that jurisdiction. Early in 1982 the District of Columbia Court of Appeals amended its disciplinary rules on vicarious disqualification.[66] The court was not willing to wait until the Kutak Commission of the American Bar Association[67] had completed its work because of its sense of the need for speedier and definitive resolution of the matter in the District of Columbia.[68]

Under the new disciplinary rules, a former government attorney may not accept private employment in any matter in which he participated personally and substantially while in government, and this disqualification extends to lawyers with whom he is associated.[69] But there is an important exception. If the disqualified former government attorney "is screened from any form of participation . . . and from sharing in any fees resulting"[70] from the employment, his colleagues are not required to decline or withdraw. There is a further requirement that the disqualified former government attorney provide the former employer and any parties in the matter with a signed document attesting to the disqualification and screening from the matter and from all fees.[71] A colleague of the former government attorney also must provide the same persons with a certification that all affiliated lawyers are aware of the screening requirement and with a description of the screening procedures to be followed.[72]

The Lawyer and her prospective employers will have to adjust their relationship to satisfy the new disciplinary rules. The rules sensibly do not impose absolute vicarious disqualification. Nevertheless, they do constitute a complication and an added burden in the relationship between the Lawyer and her new associates. Yet it is improbable that a decision on whether to hire her would turn on the existence of these rules. There may be a risk that the Lawyer will be less attractive to some potential employers because of these limits on their activities as well as hers, but she would probably be justified in the expectation that she will obtain a satisfactory position,

48

without overwhelming interference from the professional standards now in effect in the District of Columbia.

The Modesty of Direct Costs and the Immodesty of Indirect Costs

The direct costs of present ethics-in-government laws are relatively modest. Certainly various persons while in government service and after leaving it find that they are unable to do various things they might otherwise do, but these limits tend to be recognized, if not always accepted, as simply one more aspect of the restrictions on personal freedom that accompany most forms of employment. Compliance with these requirements is rather straightforward, though on occasion painful. For most they are another thing to consider and for some another report to file. The mere act of compliance is not especially burdensome, and the uncertainty accompanying compliance usually is not great. When in doubt, avoid it, divest it, or resign.

From the government's perspective also the direct costs are not significant. Added costs for enforcement and administration are not particularly high in the grand scheme of things, although they may be somewhat greater since the creation in 1978 of the Office of Government Ethics.

Indirect costs, however, though less conspicuous, may tend toward the immodest. In the hypothetical case studies, the Middle Manager cannot afford to accept the position with the Department of Labor, and the Entrepreneur and probably the Industrialist refuse to pay the price of entry: the abandonment of the personal holdings they worked diligently to accumulate.

This, of course, does not mean that the government will be left untended. Other persons having comparable background and experience may be willing to make the adjustments necessary under present laws. The Careerist, the Heir, the Professor, and probably the Lawyer will still be available. As former Treasury Secretary William Simon once observed in objecting to the implications of the 1978 act: "It is just ridiculous. We're going to end up with nothing but academics and neuters."[73] Yet even if this statement is too strong, the government has suffered a loss; its options have been limited, as some persons who presumably were its first choice have been excluded from consideration.

The assertion that the ethics-in-government laws hinder the ability of the government to attract some of the persons it desires for public service has met with skepticism. One editorial commentator noted, for example: "Now that President-elect Reagan has chosen almost all of his Cabinet, some preliminary answers emerge to a question raised by the transition workers: Does the 1978 Ethics in Government Act now make top-level recruitment too hard? To oversimplify a bit, the answer is no."[74] Others have suggested, however, that the problem is even more pronounced at "the sub-Cabinet level—where public service largely lacks the incentive of a title that 'your grandchildren will remember.' "[75]

It is on this point that empirical research would be most beneficial. To know who was lost to the government and under what circumstances would add much to the debate. But that is beyond the scope of this study, and a few examples from the popular press will have to suffice. In the future, congressional hearings on the issue would be a useful substitute for empirical research.

During the transition from the Carter to the Reagan administration there were reports of various losses. A banker declined the job of deputy energy secretary because of family oil interests. A senior vice-president of a major corporation turned down the position of under secretary of the interior because he concluded that the restrictions on the activities of a former government employee would have precluded his becoming president of his company when he returned. Another person refused the position of secretary of the interior because of conflicts with family grazing rights on federal lands.[76] The reader can decide whether these cases reflect a problem and constitute a loss to the government.

Naturally, if a person is monastic in his inclinations, has few personal needs outside his work, takes a self-imposed vow of poverty, renounces his worldly possessions, and has no family or an extremely supportive one, these matters should be of little more than academic interest. The same may be true of very wealthy persons. A few years ago the extremely wealthy son of a famous family observed during a gubernatorial race that he, unlike his opponent, had sufficient money that the public need not be concerned that he would dip into the public fisc. Both are extreme cases.

The experience of one state with ethics in government is more typical. The legislature passed a law requiring extensive disclosure of personal financial interests. A psychiatrist, facing the problem of identifying his patients by name, decided not to stand for reelection. Lawyers had the same problem concerning clients, and the number of lawyers in the legislature decreased dramatically. Some would see that as undeniably beneficial, but the indirect cost was the unavailability of such persons for public office. Federal ethics-in-government laws create the same indirect costs. Only their magnitude is unknown.

Notes

1. See section "Title 18 of the U.S. Code," in chap. 2.
2. See ibid.
3. See sections "The Ethics in Government Act of 1978" and "Executive Orders and Agency Regulations," in chap. 2.
4. See section "The Ethics in Government Act of 1978," in chap. 2.
5. See section "Executive Orders and Agency Regulations," in chap. 2.
6. 7 C.F.R. secs. 0.735–1 to –43 (1983).
7. See generally ibid., sec. 0.735–13.
8. Ibid., sec. 0.735–13(a).
9. Ibid., sec. 0.735–13(c).
10. See "The Ethics in Government Act of 1978." See also 7 C.F.R. sec. 0.735–44 (1983).
11. 7 C.F.R. sec. 0.735–31 (1981).
12. See sections "Title 18 of the U.S. Code" and "The Ethics in Government Act of 1978," in chap. 2.
13. 7 C.F.R. secs. 0.735–12(a), (c)(2) (1983).
14. Ibid., sec. 0.735–21.
15. Ibid., sec. 0.735–21(a).
16. 32 C.F.R. secs. 40.1–.25 (1983).
17. 18 U.S.C. sec. 201 (1976 & Supp. 1982).
18. 32 C.F.R. sec. 40.1 (1983).
19. Ibid., sec. 40.7(a).
20. Ibid., sec. 40.7(d).
21. Ibid., sec. 40.20.
22. Ibid., sec. 40.12.
23. 5 C.F.R. sec. 734.401(a) (1983).
24. Ibid., sec. 734.401(b)(3)(i).
25. Ibid., sec. 734.404.
26. 18 U.S.C. sec. 209(b) (1982).
27. See sections "The Ethics in Government Act of 1978" and "Executive Orders and Agency Regulations," in chap. 2 for a discussion of the Ethics in Government Act of 1978 and 32 C.F.R. secs. 40.1–25 (1983) for the Defense Department regulations.
28. 5 U.S.C. sec. 210 (App. 1982).
29. Exec. Order No. 11222, 30 Fed. Reg. 6469 (1965), as amended by Exec. Order No. 11590, 36 Fed. Reg. 7831, reprinted in 18 U.S.C. sec. 201 (1976).
30. Ibid.
31. 18 U.S.C. sec. 209(a) (1982).
32. Ibid., sec. 209(e).
33. Ibid., sec. 209(b).
34. Ibid., sec. 209(c).
35. Ibid., sec. 207(a). See 5 C.F.R. secs. 737(c)(1), –.5 (1983).
36. See 18 U.S.C. sec. 203 (1976 & Supp. 1982).
37. See 29 C.F.R. secs. 2.2 –.3 (1983).
38. 18 U.S.C. sec. 208(a) (1982).
39. Ibid., sec. 208(b).
40. See section "The Ethics in Government Act of 1978," in chap. 2.

41. 5 C.F.R. sec. 734.401(b)(3) (1982). See generally secs. 734.401–.408.

42. See 18 U.S.C. sec. 207(a) (1982).

43. See generally ibid., sec. 207 and 5 C.F.R. part 737 (1983).

44. See section "The Ethics in Government Act of 1978."

45. See 5 C.F.R. secs. 734.303(c), –.402(a)–(b) (1983).

46. Ibid., sec. 734.303.

47. Some, but of necessity by no means all, of the ethics-in-government laws apply to special government employees. These are persons who perform services for the government on a basis that is limited in both function and duration while maintaining their normal activities and occupations. Special government employees are beyond the scope of this study.

48. 18 U.S.C. sec. 209(a) (1982).

49. Ibid., sec. 207(a).

50. 5 C.F.R. sec. 737.5(c)(1) (1983).

51. 18 U.S.C. sec. 207(b)(i) (1982).

52. Ibid., sec. 207(b)(ii).

53. Ibid., sec. 207(c).

54. See 5 C.F.R. sec. 737.11(c) (1983).

55. 18 U.S.C. sec. 207(d)(2) (1982).

56. Ibid., sec. 207(f). See 5 C.F.R. sec. 737.15 (1983).

57. 18 U.S.C. sec. 207(f) (1982). See 5 C.F.R. sec. 737.17 (1983).

58. 18 U.S.C. sec. 208(a) (1983).

59. Ibid., sec. 208(b).

60. Ibid., sec. 207(a). See generally 5 C.F.R. sec. 737.5 (1983).

61. 18 U.S.C. sec. 207(b)(i) (1982). See generally 5 C.F.R. sec. 737.7 (1983).

62. See generally 18 U.S.C. secs. 207(b)(ii), (c) (1982); 5 C.F.R. secs. 737.9, 737.11 (1983).

63. 18 U.S.C. sec. 207(g) (1982).

64. 5 C.F.R. sec. 737.21(b) (1983).

65. Ibid., sec. 737.9(c).

66. "Revolving Door," 50 U.S.L.W. 2662 (D.C. Ct. App. Apr. 30, 1982) (No. M-81-88).

67. See section "Ethical Standards for Licensed Professionals as De Facto Federal Law," in chap. 2.

68. "Revolving Door," 50 U.S.L.W. 2662 (D.C. Ct. App. Apr. 4, 1982) (No. M-81-88).

69. Ibid., D.R. 9–101(B), 9–102(A).

70. Ibid., D.R. 9–102(B).

71. Ibid., D.R. 9–102(C).

72. Ibid.

73. *Time*, January 26, 1981.

74. *New York Times*, December 28, 1980.

75. *Newsweek*, December 15, 1980.

76. *Time*, January 26, 1981.

4
Conclusion

Ethics-in-Government Laws and the Quality of Government: Can Government Ever Be Too "Ethical"?

The ethics-in-government laws reflect one set of significant and worthwhile values. In great measure they serve to develop and protect public confidence in the integrity of government. It is important to note that present ethics-in-government laws do not attempt to achieve the highest conceivable standards. They are not unbending but reveal a degree of pragmatism and compromise in response to the exigencies as well as the aspirations of good government. Thus, in asking whether government can ever be too ethical, we must bear in mind that present laws are not as demanding as they might be.

To follow the implications of many of the present ethics-in-government laws, however, is to glimpse the underlying ideal of absolute ethical conduct in government service. This ideal might be reached by removing the temptations and circumstances that have led to the present legal restrictions, which afford a picture of the ideal public servant.

The ideal public servant should have no personal financial needs that the rewards he receives in return for his service cannot satisfy. There should be no need for part-time jobs to supplement his public income. And he should have no financial interests that might present conflicts. His personal finances should be simple. What he brings to government or accumulates while there should be invested in nothing more flamboyant than U.S. savings bonds.

Naturally the ideal public servant must come from somewhere, but it is preferable if he comes to the government directly after graduation from the educational system. He will then not carry with him any baggage of potential conflicts arising from prior employment and experience. Moreover, the ideal public servant should have no desire or opportunity to move out of government service for any reason other than retirement or death.

This ideal obviously does not exist. Present ethics-in-government laws fall far short of pursuing this barren absolute. Is that to be taken as an indication that present laws are inadequate or that they are, at least to a degree, "unethical"? The clear and correct answer is that it is not. Present laws merely reflect and accommodate other equally important values. Legislators may value a public service cadre that is a mixture of career employees and those who come to government for a relatively short period of time. If realization of this goal requires some relaxation in the ideal of the public servant, that does not constitute a slide toward less ethical or unethical standards. Rather it constitutes a rejection of the notion of a permanent bureaucracy and a recognition of the reality that if we value the influx of new people and ideas into government, we cannot extract a promise that they stay for life in the name of ethics and expect most of them to come.

It is thus quite possible for ethics-in-government laws to be too ethical. One may conclude, for example, that avoidance of all appearances of conflict of interest is to be valued above all else. The laws that follow will be too ethical to the extent that they sacrifice other important values. There is nothing improper in this if a consensus is reached that one value is higher than all others and is to be pursued at their expense. But if there is no single-minded commitment to a single value, something less can be expected, understood, and valued as the outcome of a competition among different and competing values. That is why present ethics-in-government laws are not in any sense "unethical" and why slightly less stringent laws would be no more so.

The importance of this cannot be overstated. The temptation in discussing ethics in government is to view any relaxation from some ideal of conduct as a subversion of the ideal and a fortiori less ethical. That view is unduly superficial; what may seem less is more accurately only different—a different value. If the other value is worthy and prevails to some extent when weighed in competition with the ideal, it is not unethical.

The danger that must be recognized and avoided is the assumption that there can never be a harmful surplus of ethics in government. In reality ethics in government are susceptible to the adverse consequences of oversupply. It is like purity in foods; as one approaches the absolute of purity in foods, the costs of each additional increment of purity rise exponentially.

A Time for Reexamination and Refinement

Obviously the goal of ethical conduct in the performance of public duties should not be abandoned. But periodic reexamination and
54

refinement of the ethics-in-government laws are reasonable and worthwhile undertakings. Today is not too soon. Ample time has passed to permit a degree of detachment from the atmosphere of Watergate without losing sight of its most important lessons. In addition, the government has had over five years and a transition in administrations to gain experience in the workings of the Ethics in Government Act of 1978.

If a reexamination does occur, a number of refinements deserve consideration. Assessment of their merits depends in great measure on certain basic assumptions, the most important of which is that a career bureaucracy, especially at the higher levels in the executive branch, is undesirable and therefore to be rejected. From this it follows that public service for less than a lifetime is to be encouraged.

In this context it is easier to recognize that federal public service is but one among many alternatives open to persons capable of serving at the higher levels of government and making substantial contributions to the quality of government. Government service competes in a wider marketplace for the services of these persons, and in the absence of a system of conscription for nonmilitary public officers and employees, their decisions to accept or reject public positions are voluntary. Consequently, ethics-in-government laws are part of a bargain; if they are unduly restrictive, no bargain will be struck, and the government will lose the services of persons it wants and needs.

With these points and principles in mind, we can consider without guilt the following areas in which the ethics-in-government laws merit reexamination and perhaps refinement. Modification of the laws need not be viewed as a sacrifice of the public interest to the cause of private gain. The ultimate interest of the government in modification of these laws may be just as great as that of private persons or even greater.

The adequacy of federal compensation is beyond the scope of this study, but it is common knowledge that compensation for those in the higher reaches of government is not fully competitive with that in the private sector. Apparently political realities make direct resolution of this problem impossible. But some change in the ethics-in-government laws could ameliorate the effects of otherwise inadequate compensation. Under the government's supervision and with its consent, the ban on other compensation for government services should be lifted. This would open the way for private sector supplementation of government wages and remove the specter of a loss in necessary income from the list of considerations of many prospective government employees.

Similarly, the 15 percent ceiling on outside earned income for high-level officers and employees should be raised or entirely eliminated. For a person with a $50,000 federal salary, the 15 percent limit is unrealistic. Such persons are likely to have the capacity for greater earnings without significant expenditures of time and effort. A government employee who has outside employment as a consultant at a rate of $100 an hour will spend little time on the outside before encountering the ceiling. The opportunity to earn more may be essential if he is to join the government and remain for a reasonable time. The only limiting factors should be that the outside activities must not jeopardize the employee's capacity to perform his government duties and must not create conflicts of interest with those duties. With these restrictions, lifting or removing the ceiling might delay the day when the employee leaves government service to put his children through college.

The financial disclosure laws should also be altered. The information that must be disclosed seems reasonable. The government has an interest in making an independent determination of the existence or appearance of improprieties and conflicts. What is less clear is the necessity for public dissemination of this information. If independent public officials review the information and take whatever action they believe necessary, the fundamental interests of the government should be protected. Admittedly, the interests of the media and some of the public would not be served, but to satisfy these interests as well is to accept certain costs.

In the last transition of administrations, it was reported that one prospective appointee for a high position withdrew upon learning of the disclosure requirements and observed: "Nobody knows how wealthy I am. I don't even want my children to know."[1] A desire to preserve privacy concerning personal affairs is not difficult to understand, and if this interest and the interests of the government can be accommodated, they should be. Public reporting without public disclosure would be an alternative middle ground. This was the approach taken before the Ethics in Government Act under Executive Order No. 11222,[2] and a return to it has merit. Otherwise we may lose the public services of persons who have nothing to hide but do have something they value—their privacy. Recalling that the Constitutional Convention managed to produce commendable results while conducting its proceedings in secrecy, we can recognize secrecy as not inevitably untoward or undesirable.

Another area for inquiry is the role of professional organizations such as bar associations in the development of standards that become de facto federal ethics-in-government laws. As others have suggested:

Problems arise . . . when the bar attempts to develop special rules that are applicable only to government attorneys. Insofar as conflict-of-interest rules for government lawyers are based on judgments about public policy and effective government rather than professional regulation alone, such choices are more appropriately made within the government as a part of the normal policymaking process. Thus, while professional standards that apply to all attorneys are the proper province of the bar associations, rules applicable to government attorneys alone are more appropriately formulated by the government entity.[3]

This reasoning is sound and justifies the conclusion that some federal preemption of the activities of professional organizations is in order to the extent that those activities purport to control the ethical conduct of government attorneys. Furthermore, there is reason to extend this approach to matters relating to the activities of former government attorneys. What is permissible after leaving government service may affect government interests as much as what is permissible while in it.

Another area of the law that warrants closer scrutiny concerns the personal interests of government officers and employees. Some thought should be given to the possibility of allowing separation of control over personal assets through a trust without insisting on divestiture. Although a trust that retains assets originally placed in it is not a blind trust, it may be too much to expect some persons to dispose of their assets to eliminate questions of conflicts of interest.

The alternative may be especially undesirable to the government. An extensive disqualification agreement may reduce the effectiveness of the employee and make divestiture the only alternative. This means that persons such as the Entrepreneur will never be able to serve in the government in matters related to their expertise. The problem is the appearance of impropriety. If disqualification were limited to actual conflicts and such persons were allowed to place their assets in trust beyond their control but without an effective mandate to divest, an accommodation might be reached that would permit government service.

The need for such accommodations is particularly acute for some. Self-made persons are likely to have assets that are concentrated in a single area or company rather than diversified; questions of the need for divestiture will be more common among them. Presumably the traits exhibited by the self-made person would be of some use to the government.

These are a few illustrative areas for reexamination and refinement. They suggest the kind of government interests that might be given greater weight than in the past in devising ethics-in-government laws. To do so might improve the quality of government. A greater pool of willing and capable talent would be available for federal public service. The disproportionate effects of the ethics-in-government laws, especially on the middle class and the private sector, would be reduced. If there are fewer barriers to entry and exit, there should be greater opportunities for excellence.

Notes

1. *Time*, January 26, 1981.

2. Exec. Order No. 11222, 30 Fed. Reg. 6469 (1965), as amended by Exec. Order No. 11590, 36 Fed. Reg. 7831, reprinted in 18 U.S.C. sec. 201 (1976).

3. Note, "Developments in the Law—Conflicts of Interest in the Legal Profession," *Harvard Law Review*, vol. 94 (1981), pp. 1244, 1443–44.